U·X·L

American Decades

1990 · 1999

Rob Nagel, Editor

U·X·L ®

THOMSON

GALE

Detroit • New York • San Diego • San Francisco • Cleveland • New Haven, Conn. • Waterville, Maine • London • Munich

U•X•L American Decades, 1990–1999

Rob Nagel, Editor

Project Editors
Diane Sawinski, Julie L. Carnagie, and Christine Slovey

Editorial
Elizabeth Anderson

Permissions
Shalice Shah-Caldwell

Imaging and Multimedia
Dean Dauphinais

Product Design
Pamela A.E. Galbreath

Composition
Evi Seoud

Manufacturing
Rita Wimberley

For permission to use material from this product, submit your request via Web at http://www.gale-edit.com/permissions, or you may download our Permissions Request form and submit your request by fax or mail to:

Permissions Department
The Gale Group, Inc.
27500 Drake Rd.
Farmington Hills, MI 48331-3535
Permissions Hotline:
248-699-8006 or 800-877-4253, ext. 8006
Fax: 248-699-8074 or 800-762-4058

Cover photograph reproduced by permission of the Corbis Corporation.

While every effort has been made to ensure the reliability of the information presented in this publication, The Gale Group, Inc. does not guarantee the accuracy of the data contained herein. The Gale Group, Inc. accepts no payment for listing; and inclusion in the publication of any organization, agency, institution, publication, service, or individual does not imply endorsement of the editors or publisher. Errors brought to the attention of the publisher and verified to the satisfaction of the publisher will be corrected in future editions.

Vol. 1: 0-7876-6455-3
Vol. 2: 0-7876-6456-1
Vol. 3: 0-7876-6457-X
Vol. 4: 0-7876-6458-8
Vol. 5: 0-7876-6459-6
Vol. 6: 0-7876-6460-X
Vol. 7: 0-7876-6461-8
Vol. 8: 0-7876-6462-6
Vol. 9: 0-7876-6463-4
Vol. 10: 0-7876-6464-2

LIBRARY OF CONGRESS CATALOGING-IN-PUBLICATION DATA

U•X•L American decades
    p. cm.
Includes bibliographical references and index.
    Contents: v. 1. 1900-1910—v. 2. 1910-1919—v. 3.1920-1929—v. 4. 1930-1939—v. 5. 1940-1949—v. 6. 1950-1959—v. 7. 1960-1969—v. 8. 1970-1979—v. 9.1980-1989—v. 10. 1990-1999.
    Summary: A ten-volume overview of the twentieth century which explores such topics as the arts, economy, education, government, politics, fashions, health, science, technology, and sports which characterize each decade.
    ISBN 0-7876-6454-5 (set: hardcover: alk. paper)
    1. United States—Civilization—20th century—Juvenile literature. 2. United States—History—20th century—Juvenile literature. [1. United States—Civilization—20th century. 2. United States—History—20th century.] I. UXL (Firm) II. Title: UXL American decades. III. Title: American decades.
E169.1.U88 2003
973.91—dc21
2002010176

Contents

chapter four *Government, Politics, and Law* . 61

Reader's Guide

U•X•L American Decades provides a broad overview of the major events and people that helped to shape American society throughout the twentieth century. Each volume in this ten-volume set chronicles a single decade and begins with an introduction to that decade and a timeline of major events in twentieth-century America. Following are eight chapters devoted to these categories of American endeavor:

• Arts and Entertainment

• Business and the Economy

• Education

• Government, Politics, and Law

• Lifestyles and Social Trends

• Medicine and Health

• Science and Technology

• Sports

These chapters are then divided into five sections:

Chronology: A timeline of significant events within the chapter's particular field.

❋ **Overview:** A summary of the events and people detailed in that chapter.

★ **Headline Makers:** Short biographical accounts of key people and their achievements during the decade.

❖ **Topics in the News:** A series of short topical essays describing events and people within the chapter's theme.

✛ **For More Information:** A section that lists books and Web sites directing the student to further information about the events and people covered in the chapter.

OTHER FEATURES

Each volume of *U•X•L American Decades* contains more than eighty black-and-white photographs and illustrations that bring the events and people discussed to life and sidebar boxes that expand on items of high interest to readers. Concluding each volume is a general bibliography of books and Web sites that explore the particular decade in general and a thorough subject index that allows readers to easily locate the events, people, and places discussed throughout that volume of *U•X•L American Decades*.

COMMENTS AND SUGGESTIONS

We welcome your comments on *U•X•L American Decades* and suggestions for other history topics to consider. Please write: Editors, *U•X•L American Decades,* U•X•L, 27500 Drake Rd., Farmington Hills, MI 48331-3535; call toll-free: 1-800-877-4253; fax: 248-699-8097; or send e-mail via http://www.galegroup.com.

Chronology of the 1990s

1990:   **January 1** Maryland becomes the first state to ban the sale of cheap handguns known as Saturday Night Specials.

1990:   **January 10** Warner Communications and Time Inc. complete a $14.1 billion merger, establishing the largest media conglomerate in the world.

1990:   **March 5** Channel One, a commercially sponsored television news program designed for use in high-school classrooms, makes its formal debut in four hundred schools across the country.

1990:   **March 9** Antonia Novello becomes the first woman and the first Hispanic American U.S. Surgeon General.

1990:   **April 12** Under pressure from environmental groups, three top U.S. canneries implement "dolphin-safe" tuna-catching practices.

1990:   **April 24** The Hubble Space Telescope is placed into orbit by the space shuttle *Discovery*.

1990:   **June 11** Nolan Ryan of the Texas Rangers pitches his sixth no-hit game, a major league baseball record, against the Oakland Athletics.

1990:   **August 2** Saddam Hussein's Iraqi army seizes Kuwait; President George H. W. Bush freezes Iraqi and Kuwaiti assets in U.S. financial institutions; the United Nations calls on Iraq to withdraw.

1990: September 14 U.S. geneticist W. French Anderson performs the first gene therapy on a human, injecting engineered genes into a four-year-old child to repair her faulty immune system.

1990: October 1 The Human Genome Project is formally launched.

1990: November 1 Under pressure from environmental groups, McDonald's agrees to replace styrofoam containers with paper wrappers.

1990: December The U.S. Congress requires that artists funded by the National Endowment for the Arts must return grant money if their works are judged obscene.

1991: The CDC releases a report based on a 1990 survey that found that almost one in five American high-school students sometimes carried a gun, knife, or other weapon to school.

1991: January 16 U.S. warplanes and missiles attack Iraq and occupy Kuwait in Operation Desert Storm.

1991: February 14 Homosexual and unmarried heterosexual couples begin registering under a new law in San Francisco to be recognized as "domestic partners."

1991: March 3 Rodney King is beaten by Los Angeles police officers following a high-speed automobile chase.

1991: July 3 Apple Computer and IBM publicly join together in an effort to exchange technologies and develop new equipment.

1991: July 15 Sandhi Ortiz-DelValle becomes the first woman to officiate a men's professional basketball game.

1991: October 11 The Anita Hill-Clarence Thomas hearings begin before the U.S. Senate Judiciary Committee. Hill accused the Supreme Court nominee of sexual harassment.

1991: November 20 Jack Kevorkian's medical license is suspended in Michigan in hopes of preventing him from assisting in any more patient suicides.

1992: General Motors announces a record $4.5 billion loss in 1991 and says it will close twenty-one plants and lay off some seventy-four thousand workers it the next four years.

1992: Compact discs surpass cassette tapes as the preferred medium for recorded music.

1992: February 1 President Bush and Russian President Boris Yeltsin proclaim a formal end to the cold war.

1992: **April 29** Rioting erupts in South Central Los Angeles after four police officers accused of beating Rodney King are either acquitted or given light sentences. The rioting lasts until May 2.

1992: **June 24** The U.S. Supreme Court rules five to four that prayers delivered at a public high school graduation violated First Amendment principles separating church and state.

1992: **August 11** The Mall of America, the biggest shopping complex built in the United States, opens in Bloomington, Minnesota.

1992: **December 24** As his term in office nears an end, President Bush pardons all former Reagan officials who were involved in the Iran-Contra scandal in the mid-1980s.

1993: Writer Toni Morrison is awarded the Nobel Prize for literature, becoming the first African American woman to receive the distinguished honor.

1993: Director Steven Spielberg releases *Schindler's List,* a film about the Holocaust. Many critics proclaim it the best movie of the decade.

1993: **February 26** The World Trade Center in New York City is bombed, killing six people and injuring more than one thousand. Several Islamic extremists are later arrested and convicted for the attack.

1993: **April 19** A fifty-one-day siege by federal agents of the Branch Davidian compound near Waco, Texas, ends in a fiery inferno, killing almost eighty men, women, and children.

1993: **September 6** The "Doomsday 2000" article, warning about possible Y2K (Year 2000) problems, is published in *Computerworld* by Canadian Peter de Jager.

1993: **September 8** Joycelyn Elders becomes the first African American U.S. Surgeon General.

1993: **October 27** Embryologist Jerry Hall of George Washington University reports the first cloning of a human embryo.

1993: **October 27** President Bill Clinton's 1,342-page Health Plan is delivered to the U.S. Congress.

1994: **January 1** The North American Free Trade Agreement goes into effect.

1994: **February 3** President Clinton ends the trade embargo against the Republic of Vietnam, which had been put into effect in 1975.

1994: **May 6** Paula Corbin Jones files suit in federal court charging President Clinton with having committed sexual harassment against her while he was governor of Arkansas.

1994: **June 17** O. J. Simpson is charged with the murder of his former wife Nicole Brown Simpson and her friend Ronald Goldman. Media helicopters televise Simpson's flight from the police in a white Ford Bronco along a Los Angeles freeway.

1994: **July 15** In a settlement with the U.S. Justice Department, Microsoft promises to end practices used to corner the personal computer software program market.

1994: **August 12** Major league baseball players go on strike to protest the owners' plan for a salary cap. The season is ended and the World Series is canceled for the first time in ninety years.

1994: **August 12 to 14** Woodstock '94 commemorates the twenty-fifth anniversary of the original week-end-long concert held near Woodstock, New York.

1994: **October 11** The Colorado Supreme Court strikes down an antigay-rights measures as unconstitutional.

1994: **November** In an open letter to the American public, former president Ronald Reagan announces that he has Alzheimer's disease.

1994: **December 15** Netscape Communications Corporation releases its graphical browser, Netscape Navigator 1.0, initiating a communications revolution. Within four months, 75 percent of all Internet users are accessing the Web using this browser.

1994: **December 15** The U.S. Food and Drug Administration (FDA) permits the first U.S. test of RU-486, an abortion-inducing pill, in Des Moines, Iowa.

1995: **March** The FDA approves the first U.S. vaccine to prevent chicken pox, a childhood disease afflicting 3.7 million people each year.

1995: **March 19** Michael Jordan, who had retired the previous year to play baseball for the Chicago White Sox, returns to professional basketball to play for the Chicago Bulls.

1995: **April 19** A bomb explodes at the Alfred P. Murrah Federal Building in Oklahoma City, Oklahoma, killing 168 people and injuring more than 500.

1995: **June 21** The Southern Baptist Convention formally apologizes for its history of racism.

1995: **August 12** Shannon Faulkner becomes the first woman to attend The Citadel in Charleston, South Carolina, as a member of its Corps of Cadets. She drops out of the school six days later.

1995: **September 1** The Rock and Roll Hall of Fame and Museum, designed by architect I. M. Pei, opens in Cleveland, Ohio.

1995: **September 6** Cal Ripken Jr., an infielder for the Baltimore Orioles, plays in his 2,131st consecutive major league baseball game, breaking Lou Gehrig's record.

1995: **October 3** O. J. Simpson is acquitted of the murders of his former wife Nicole Brown Simpson and her friend Ronald Goldman.

1995: **October 16** Nation of Islam leader Louis Farrakhan leads the Million Man March in Washington, D.C.

1996: The first genetically engineered insect, a predator mite that researchers hope will eat other mites that damage strawberries and other crops, is released in Florida.

1996: **January 26** First Lady Hillary Rodham Clinton testifies before a grand jury in connection with the Whitewater investigation

1996: **April 3** Theodore "Ted" Kaczynski is arrested by FBI agents at his Montana cabin in connection with the Unabomber case.

1996: **July 12** The U.S. House of Representatives votes overwhelmingly to define marriage in federal laws as the legal union of men and women only, regardless of what individual states recognize.

1996: **September 13** Rapper Tupac Shakur dies six days after having been shot by two gunmen while sitting in a car in traffic in Las Vegas.

1996: **September 25** NASA biochemist Shannon Lucid returns home after spending six months aboard the Russian space station *Mir*, earning her the title of America's most experienced astronaut.

1996: **November 15** Texaco settles a racial discrimination lawsuit, agreeing to pay more than $140 million, a record for racial discrimination cases, in light of reports that tapes existed in which executives were caught making disparaging remarks about minorities and were planning to destroy incriminating evidence.

1996: **December 5** President Clinton appoints Madeleine Albright as the first female Secretary of State.

1997: Driver and passenger side airbags are required to be installed in all new cars.

1997: **January 1** David Da-I Ho is named "Man of the Year" by *Time* magazine for his AIDS research.

1997: **February 8** President Clinton announces the first in Department of Education grants to public schools to help them connect to the Internet.

1997: **March 9** Rap star Notorious B.I.G. is killed in Los Angeles as he is leaving a music industry party. No one was ever arrested for the crime.

1997: **March 26** Thirty-nine members of the Heaven's Gate religious cult commit suicide in their home near San Diego, California. They anticipated being taken to a higher level of being in a flying saucer supposedly trailing the Hale-Bopp comet.

1997: **April 9** Golfer Tiger Woods wins the Masters tournament with a record eighteen-under-par.

1997: **June 2** Timothy McVeigh is convicted of charges in connection with the Murrah Federal Building bombing in Oklahoma City.

1997: **June 28** Evander Holyfield wins a heavyweight fight against Mike Tyson when Tyson is disqualified for biting his opponent's ear.

1997: **October 28** Dee Kantner and Violet Palmer make history by becoming the first female referees in the NBA.

1997: **December 19** *Titanic* opens in American movie theaters. The most expensive movie ever made, it cost $300 million to produce and market.

1998: J. Craig Venter, with his private research company Celera Genomics, announces plans to decode the entire human genome by 2001, years ahead of the Human Genome Project deadline.

1998: With a market value of more than $260 billion, Microsoft passes General Electric as the biggest company in the United States.

1998: **January 21** President Clinton denies an alleged affair with former White House intern Monica Lewinsky.

1998: **June 25** The U.S. Supreme Court rules that the National Endowment for the Arts could consider general standards of decency when making grants.

1998: **September 8** Mark McGwire of the St. Louis Cardinals breaks Roger Maris's single-season home run record, hitting number sixty-two.

1998: **October 16** Antigay protestors demonstrate outside the funeral of twenty-one-year-old Matthew Wayne Shepard, a gay student at the University of Wyoming who died October 12 after having been beaten on October 7.

1998: **October 29** The space shuttle *Discovery* launches with seventy-seven-year-old U.S. senator and former astronaut John Glenn aboard as a payload specialist.

1998: **December 1** The largest U.S. oil company, Exxon, announces it will buy the second largest oil company, Mobil, for $80 billion, forming the largest corporation in the world.

1998: **December 19** The U.S. House of Representatives passes two Articles of Impeachment against President Clinton.

1999: **January 7** The U.S. Senate impeachment trial of President Clinton begins with Chief Justice William Rehnquist presiding.

1999: **February 9** Reverend Jerry Falwell warns in his *National Liberty Journal* that Tinky-Winky, a character on the popular children's television program *Teletubbies*, promotes a homosexual lifestyle.

1999: **February 12** President Clinton is acquitted on both Articles of Impeachment.

1999: **March 26** Jack Kevorkian is found guilty of second-degree murder and the delivery of a controlled substance by a Michigan jury and is sentenced to serve ten to twenty-five years in prison.

1999: **April 12** A U.S. district court judge holds President Clinton in contempt of court for giving misleading information when he was asked about his relationship with Monica Lewinsky. It is the first time in U.S. history a sitting president is held in contempt of civil court.

1999: **April 20** At Columbine High School in Littleton. Colorado, two boys shoot and kill twelve fellow students and a teacher, and wound more than twenty other classmates before committing suicide.

1999: **May 3** The Dow Jones Industrial Average closes about 11,000 only twenty-four trading days after breaking the 10,000 mark, making it the fastest ride in history.

1999: **July 14** *The Blair Witch Project* is released, becoming a cult-movie classic and grossing more than $140 million. Because the production cost of the movie was only $30 thousand, it is the most profitable film ever made.

1999: July 25 Cyclist Lance Armstrong makes an amazing comeback after battling testicular cancer to win the Tour de France, the world's premiere cycling event.

1999: August 11 The Kansas State Board of Education decides that the state will no longer test students on evolution, though it still may be taught.

1999: December 1 Scientists from the United States, Japan, and England announce the first mapping of an entire human genome, part of the Human Genome Project.

1999: December 26 Michael Jordan is selected by the Entertainment and Sports Programming Network (ESPN) as the greatest North American athlete of the twentieth century.

The 1990s: An Overview

The decade of the 1990s began with great hope for Americans: the Soviet Union dissolved and Iraq was defeated in the 1990–91 Persian Gulf War. Yet that hope was not long-lasting. Although the fear of a global thermonuclear war with the Soviet Union had been removed, it was soon replaced by the fear of a regional nuclear war involving India, Pakistan, Israel, North Korea, or some shadowy terrorist group. In Iraq, Saddam Hussein, though defeated militarily, still clung defiantly to power. In the former communist state of Yugoslavia, national and religious rivalries that had been suppressed under communism reemerged with a level of violence not seen in Europe since World War II (1939–45). Similar conflicts arose in Africa and elsewhere, and the United States tried desperately and often without success to keep the peace as the world's policeman.

In this chaotic world, Americans found stability at home. For most people in the country, the decade was a time of plentiful employment opportunities. Democrat Bill Clinton served two successful terms as president because the economy prospered, inflation stayed in check, and virtually anyone who wanted a job could find one. Clinton defined himself as a New Democrat, which meant that on occasion his fiscal and trade policies had more in common with Republicans than with his Democratic predecessors. Such economic moderation played well in the 1990s.

Despite such agreement on the economy, relations between Republicans and Democrats remained bitter throughout the decade. Especially harsh were Republican attacks on Clinton. Since they could not criticize his stance on the economy, they sought to hammer him on his character.

His personal blunders, including his affair with a White House intern and his consequent lying under oath about the incident, gave the Republicans in the U.S. House of Representatives all they needed to bring impeachment charges against him. Only the second U.S. president ever to be impeached (Andrew Johnson had been the first in 1868), Clinton survived the vote in the U.S. Senate that would have resulted in his removal from office. U.S. voters, meanwhile, chose to ignore the scandal and the political posturing, approving of the job Clinton was doing.

Beyond the economy, technological innovations had the greatest impact on American society in the 1990s. Personal computers, the Internet, and genetic engineering were all products of long, painstaking work on the part of thousands of scientists and engineers over the previous decades. The changes brought about by these innovations were momentous. Computers had started to displace typewriters in American offices during the 1980s. By 1999, the once-familiar clickety-clack of typing had been silenced, replaced by the plastic sounds of computer keyboards. E-mail replaced pen-and-paper correspondence. Cellular phones and pagers made their presence known in restaurants, movie theaters, and other public venues.

Although the Internet had existed for decades as a way for computers to communicate with each other, the development in the early 1990s of the World Wide Web, easy-to-use operating systems and other computer programs, and cheaper and more powerful computers gave millions of Americans a way to send e-mail, download music, or buy products such as books online. The purpose and function of computers had changed: no longer were they used just to compute, but to communicate, advertise, and sell. In the process, they altered not only American society but almost every other one around the world.

If the 1980s was the decade to dress for success, the 1990s was a time for going casually to work and unkempt just about everywhere else. Like so much in the 1990s, it all started with the computer and Internet industry. The highly skilled and creative designers, programmers, and engineers at Microsoft, Apple, Adobe, and hundreds of Internet start-up companies had never bothered to learn to wear a tie. Since they dominated the economy, and their value was in what they knew how to do and not how they looked, they started showing up for work wearing pretty much what they pleased. The rest of the country soon followed suit.

Beneath this relaxed atmosphere, there lurked a growing terror movement, both domestic and foreign. The seventeen-year bombing spree of the Unabomber; the fifty-one-day standoff between federal agents and the Branch Davidians in 1993; the bombing of the World Trade Center in New York City that same year; the 1995 bombing of the Alfred P. Murrah Federal Building in Oklahoma City, Oklahoma; the bombing in the Olympic Centennial Park in Atlanta, Georgia, in 1996; the bombing of abortion clinics and the shooting of abortion doctors throughout the decade; and the rise of school shootings across the nation left Americans wondering how to prevent such random violence that threatened American security. Unfortunately, these events that marked the final decade of the twentieth century gave Americans but a glimpse of a world that would be forever changed at the beginning of the next millennium.

Arts and Entertainment

1990: **May 30** The sitcom *Seinfeld,* a show about "nothing," begins its highly successful eight-year run.

1990: **October 5** The Contemporary Arts Center in Cincinnati and its director, Dennis Barrie, are found not guilty of obscenity charges stemming from the exhibition of controversial photographs by Robert Mapplethorpe.

1990: **December** The U.S. Congress requires that artists funded by the National Endowment for the Arts must return grant money if their works are judged obscene.

1991: John Grisham's *The Firm,* his second novel, is published. Previously rejected by numerous publishers, the novel remains on the *New York Times* bestseller list for forty-seven weeks.

1991: **September 24** The Seattle grunge band Nirvana releases *Nevermind.* By January 11, 1992, a song from the album, "Smells Like Teen Spirit," has reached number one on the *Billboard* singles charts and has become an alternative rock anthem for Generation X.

1992: Robert James Waller's *The Bridges of Madison County* is published and becomes a sensation, much to the dismay of literary critics.

1992: Compact discs surpass cassette tapes as the preferred medium for recorded music.

1993: Writer Toni Morrison is awarded the Nobel Prize for Literature, becoming the first African American woman to receive the distinguished honor.

1993: Director Steven Spielberg releases *Schindler's List,* a film about the Holocaust. Many critics proclaim it the best movie of the decade.

1994: **April 8** The body of Nirvana lead singer Kurt Cobain is discovered in his garage. Authorities determine he had died three days earlier of a self-inflicted shotgun wound.

1994: **June 17** O. J. Simpson is charged with the murder of his ex-wife Nicole Brown Simpson and her friend Ronald Goldman. Media helicopters televise Simpson's flight from the police in a white Ford Bronco along a Los Angeles freeway.

1994: **August 12 to 14** Woodstock '94 commemorates the twenty-fifth anniversary of the original weekend-long concert held near Woodstock, New York.

1995: **March** Jonathan Schmitz shoots and kills Scott Amedure three days after the pair appeared on the *Jenny Jones Show* in an episode about secret admirers.

1995: **September 1** The Rock and Roll Hall of Fame and Museum, designed by architect I. M. Pei, opens in Cleveland.

1996: **February 8** President Bill Clinton signs the Telecommunications Reform Act, which mandates that a V-Chip be installed in every new television set.

1996: **September** Television talk-show host Oprah Winfrey announces the beginning of Oprah's Book Club. The first work chosen is *The Deep End of the Ocean* by Jacquelyn Mitchard.

1996: **September 13** Rapper Tupac Shakur dies six days after having been shot while sitting in a car in traffic in Las Vegas, Nevada.

1997: **March 9** Rap star Notorious B.I.G. is killed in Los Angeles as he is leaving a music industry party. No one is ever arrested for the crime.

1997: **December 19** *Titanic* opens in American movie theaters. The most expensive movie ever made, it costs $300 million to produce and market, yet it

eventually becomes the highest-grossing film in history.

1998: Radio "shock jock" Howard Stern begins hosting a nightly television show on E! Entertainment Television. Critics call the raunchy show "the low point in television history."

1998: Jennifer Lopez is paid $2 million for her role in the film *Out of Sight,* making her the highest-paid Latina actress in history.

1998: **June 25** The U.S. Supreme Court rules that the National Endowment for the Arts could consider general standards of decency when making grants.

1999: **May 19** *Stars War: Episode I—The Phantom Menace* is released and breaks a string of box-office records. The movie grosses $102.7 million in five days.

1999: **July 14** *The Blair Witch Project* is released, becoming a cult-movie classic and grossing more than $140 million. Because the production cost of the movies was only thirty thousand dollars, it is the most profitable movie ever made.

✳ Overview

The culture war that began in the 1980s, pitting outraged politicians against artists whose works the politicians considered obscene and the government agencies that supported them, extended into the next decade. In 1990, in the midst of calls to abolish the National Endowment for the Arts (NEA; independent federal government agency that awards grants to artists and art organizations across the country), the U.S. Congress cut the NEA's budget. Congress then went further, requiring that works by government-funded artists adhere to community standards of decency. Artists countered that such conditions discouraged creativity, and some even sued the NEA. Although the U.S. Supreme Court ultimately sided with the federal government, artists continued to offer social and political commentary in disturbing works that managed to offend some Americans.

Filmmakers in the decade also experimented with previously taboo subjects. Vulgarity and violence, designed to shock and excite, appeared in more and more movies. Even critically praised movies such as *Pulp Fiction* (1994) and *Saving Private Ryan* (1998) were violent. Yet, in this atmosphere of violence, certain films stood out with their sensitive, poetic rendering of powerful moments in history. One such film was *Schindler's List* (1993), a movie about the Holocaust, the mass murder of Jews by the Nazis during World War II (1939–45).

The shock factor in the decade was not limited to theaters. From radio to television, talk-show hosts and their audiences raised their voices and lowered the standards of acceptable social behavior. Talk radio often generated extreme emotion and misinformation. Rush Limbaugh's variety of political conservatism appealed mostly to antifeminist, anti-environmentalist, white, Republican listeners, while Laura Schlessinger pandered to troubled people needing a quick fix. Probably the greatest trash-monger of them all, however, was Howard Stern, a radio "shock jock" (disc jockey who specializes in on-air vulgarity).

Television talk shows sunk to a new low when they moved from exploring controversial subjects to initiating confrontation. Day after day, guests appeared to air their grievances with friends and lovers, while hosts and producers encouraged louder and more vicious arguments to keep the shows lively. The worst result was a murder following the taping of one *Jenny Jones Show,* in which a young man revealed his crush on his male neighbor.

The popular-music industry of the 1990s was dominated by the teen or Generation X market, with grunge rock and "gangsta" rap taking the lead. The music was loud, with abrasive and painful lyrics, depicting troubled and hopeless lives. All too often during the decade, that pain tragically snuffed out the lives of young artists speaking for their generation. Perhaps seeking a release from the tension-filled times, many music listeners also found pleasure in the songs of love and longing by pop singer and songwriter Mariah Carey. She had more number-one hits than any other female vocalist, and only eight fewer than Elvis Presley, the all-time leader.

Readers also sought to escape, buying the mystery and crime fiction of novelists such as John Grisham and Robert B. Parker. The work of Grisham, in particular, ruled the best-seller lists for most of the decade, and no other writer could crack the top spot. Book clubs across the nation helped spread the popularity of reading, and a book club started by talk-show host Oprah Winfrey did much to keep the trend alive. Literary novelists such as Cormac McCarthy, E. Annie Proulx, and Peter Matthiessen, though not as popular in the decade, produced lyrical works that received deserved acclaim. Toni Morrison, whose deeply felt works had captivated readers since the 1970s, was awarded the 1993 Nobel Prize in Literature.

Kurt Cobain (1967–1994) Kurt Cobain, guitarist and lead singer for the rock band Nirvana, helped change the course of rock-and-roll. He and his bandmates, along with a few other groups, ushered in the era of grunge, a mix of punk and heavy metal that dominated the rock music world for most of the decade. More than anyone, however, Cobain represented his generation's longing. His voice, a painful yell that started somewhere around his stomach, was instantly recognizable as that of frustrated youth. When he died of a self-inflicted gunshot wound, many thought the grunge era had come to an end. *Photo reproduced by permission of Ken Settle.*

Karen Finley (c. 1956–) Karen Finley used her performance art to comment on the abuse and oppression of women, minorities, homosexuals, AIDS victims, and the homeless. She screamed, howled, and ranted her way through confrontational pieces, often appearing nude on stage. In the early 1990s, Finley found herself at the center of a national debate over arts funding by the federal government. When her funding was denied because some members of Congress deemed her work indecent, Finley sued, taking her case to the U.S. Supreme Court. She eventually lost the case but gained publicity in the process. *Photo reproduced by permission of AP/Wide World Photos.*

John Grisham (1955–) John Grisham, the best-selling author of the 1990s, is considered by some to be the most successful author in the history of the book-publishing business. Trained as a lawyer, Grisham published his first book, *A Time to Kill,* in 1989. His second work, *The Firm* (1991), made him an overnight sensation. Grisham then wrote a best-selling legal thriller every year during the decade, capturing the top spot each of the last six years. Many of his works were also made into motion pictures that grossed millions of dollars at the box office. *Photo reproduced by permission of Archive/Capri/Saga.*

Jennifer Lopez (1970–) Jennifer Lopez received her big break in 1990 when she won a dance contest to become a Fly Girl on the Fox television comedy series *In Living Color.* Five years later, she appeared on the big screen in *Money Train.* In 1997, she made headlines by portraying the role of Tejano singing star Selena. The following year, she earned two million dollars—the highest salary ever paid to a Latina actress—for appearing in *Out of Sight.* At decade's end, she launched a singing career that matched her success in films. *Photo reproduced by permission of the Corbis Corporation.*

Laura Schlessinger (1947–) Laura Schlessinger was one of the top radio talk show hosts of the 1990s. For three hours every day, she dispensed advice while pointing out the shortcomings of the people who called in to her radio show. Armed with a doctorate in physiology and a license in marriage and family counseling, Schlessinger offered her opinions on marriage, abortion, relationships, homosexuality, and a host of other topics. Her no-holds-barred approach led many to label her an insensitive imposter, but it also earned her millions of devoted listeners.

Photo reproduced by permission of AP/Wide World Photos.

Tupac Shakur (1971–1996) Rap musician Tupac Shakur made many people uncomfortable. With his tattoo-splattered physique, piercing deep-set eyes, and shaved head, he came across as middle America's worst nightmare—the darkest strain of hip-hop. But to millions of fans, the rap star's troubled life and lyrics offered something meaningful. In a life filled with conflict and violence, Shakur showed a flair for performing. Yet, despite increasing record sales and acclaimed film roles, Shakur could not escape his violent past. Already shot once by unknown rivals, Shakur was eventually killed by two gunmen while stuck in traffic in Las Vegas, Nevada. *Photo reproduced by permission of Death Row Records.*

Quentin Tarantino (1963–) Quentin Tarantino burst onto the movie scene in 1992 with his shockingly violent, critically acclaimed movie *Reservoir Dogs*. He not only wrote and directed the film but also acted in a small role. He repeated his feat two years later with his biggest hit film of the decade, *Pulp Fiction*. Critics championed the movie despite the explicit violence. They noted that, unlike typical action films, Tarantino's movies contain dialogue that takes viewers inside the minds of the characters.

Photo reproduced by permission of AP/Wide World Photos.

Oprah Winfrey (1954–) Oprah Winfrey revolutionized the television industry as the first African American woman to own her own production company. First broadcast in 1986, her syndicated show reigned the airwaves as the number-one talk show for twelve consecutive seasons, boasting an audience of thirty-three million American viewers every weekday. Her appeal resulted from blending public dialogue and private conversation in such a way that viewers, especially women, felt they were her friends. In 1999, Winfrey's fortune was estimated at $725 million, placing her among America's wealthiest people. *Photo reproduced by permission of AP/Wide World Photos.*

❖❖❖ *Topics in the News* •

❖ ARTS AND POLITICS: CONTROVERSY AND CUTBACKS

The National Endowment for the Arts (NEA), an independent federal government agency created by the U.S. Congress in 1965, provides grants to artists, museums, and galleries to encourage promising artists who are unlikely to attract large audiences or private funding. In the late 1980s, controversy erupted in Congress over the NEA's support for certain artists, particularly photographers Andres Serrano and Robert Mapplethorpe, whose works some people found obscene or immoral. For months, certain members of Congress, led by Senator Jesse Helms from North Carolina, heavily criticized the NEA for funding such art with taxpayers' money.

In the fall of 1989, when Congress passed the annual appropriations bill determining how much money the NEA would receive from the federal government, it specified that no NEA funding could be used to promote or produce art that may be considered obscene. When Congress passed the next annual funding bill in December 1990, it specified that obscenity should be defined in accordance with community standards of decency and that artists whose work was judged obscene must return their NEA grant money.

In the midst of the debate surrounding the NEA, an exhibit of photographs by Mapplethorpe toured several cities, where it was shown without incident. When it reached the Contemporary Arts Center (CAC) in Cincinnati on April 7, 1990, however, the Hamilton County sheriff's department shut down the museum. The CAC and its director, Dennis Barrie, were subsequently prosecuted on obscenity charges. On October 5, they were found not guilty.

While arts supporters were applauding the court decision in Cincinnati as a victory for freedom of expression, a long battle over NEA funding was brewing. When the controversial performance artists Holly Hughes, John Fleck, Tim Miller, and Karen Finley (all of whom had previously received small NEA grants) applied for new NEA funding, they were recommended for grants by an initial screening panel. The director of the NEA, however, vetoed funding for the four artists because of the nature of their work. In turn, the four artists sued the NEA, arguing that the new NEA standards, among other things, represented an effort to limit freedom of expression. Finley's suit went all the way to the U.S. Supreme Court. In June 1998, the Court ruled that the NEA could indeed consider general standards of decency when making grants. The refusal to fund Finley's work did not limit her freedom to create, the Court stated.

Throughout the 1990s, the NEA suffered from budget cuts. In 1996, Congress slashed NEA funding even further, eliminating fellowships for all artists except folk artists, jazz musicians, and writers. It also cut off funding to theaters and museums. Artists faced other financial challenges later in the decade when large corporations, which had relied on the NEA to indicate artists worthy of financing, decided to withhold money they previously had offered in support of the arts.

❖ FILMS: VIOLENCE, POLITICS, AND HISTORY

In the movies of the 1990s, violence was more prevalent and graphic than ever before, and it seemed to be celebrated in a deliberately enticing manner. Many educators, politicians, and even some filmmakers expressed concerns about a possible connection between violence on the screen and increasing violent behavior in schools and on the streets. Director Oliver Stone's 1994 film, *Natural Born Killers,* in which a pair of criminals go on a murder spree in order to become famous, was intended to depict American society's obsession with violence and celebrity. After the film's release, however, teenaged murderers around the world claimed to have been inspired by the movie. Social critics pointed out that the staging of the April 1999 shootings at Columbine High School in Colorado was similar to those in *The Basketball Diaries* (1995), a film in which a trench-coat-clad young man with a machine gun attacks people who had mocked him.

Controversial photographer Robert Mapplethorpe. © Andre Grossman/Corbis. Reproduced by permission of the Corbis Corporation.

One of the most critically acclaimed movies of 1994 seemed to raise the threshold of acceptable screen violence. Director Quentin Tarantino's *Pulp Fiction* was an outrageous comedy filled with profanity, senseless shootings and stabbings, and drug overdoses. The movie contained one explicitly violent scene after another, designed to shock unsuspecting audiences. Tarantino conceived the movie as a tribute to pulp magazine stories from the 1930s and 1940s about hard-boiled detectives who survive in an amoral world by being as tough and ruthless as the criminals they are trying to defeat. While some film critics took Tarantino to task for the film's violence, many others praised the movie's artistry.

Top Films of 1990s

Year	Film
1990	Home Alone
1991	Terminator 2: Judgment Day
1992	Aladdin
1993	Jurassic Park
1994	Forrest Gump
1995	Toy Story
1996	Independence Day
1997	Titanic
1998	Saving Private Ryan
1999	Star Wars: Episode I—The Phantom Menace

By the mid-1990s, politicians had begun to target movie violence, attacking the entertainment industry in the process. The U.S. Congress proposed various bills: to ban sales of violent materials to minors, to require the entertainment industry to label violent products with government-approved warnings, and to keep filmmakers from using federal property as a setting for violent purposes. Critics of such legislation pointed out that these measures might appeal to voters but would have very little impact on the movie industry.

While the federal government was trying to regulate the movie industry, certain filmmakers were creating movies that depicted American politics in a negative light. Foremost among these was director Oliver Stone. In 1991, he released *JFK,* a $40 million movie that revived conspiracy theories about the 1963 assassination of President John F. Kennedy (1917–1963). The movie proposed that various financial and government leaders conspired to assassinate Kennedy because he was planning to pull U.S. troops out of the Vietnam War (1954–75). Stone combined computer animation with real news footage in the film, which prompted some journalists and historians to express concerns that viewers might confuse fact and fiction. Stone's follow-up film, *Nixon* (1995), raised further worries about the director manipulating historical truths to fit his artistic purposes.

A scene from the 1993 film Schindler's List. *Reproduced by permission of The Kobol Collection.*

Not all 1990s movies were cynical about American politics and history. *Forrest Gump,* one of the most popular movies of 1994, starred Tom Hanks as an intellectually impaired man who participates in every major event in American history over four decades. Critics praised the movie, pointing out that its real theme is Forrest Gump's life-affirming power to transform the lives of those around him.

Popular director Steven Spielberg made two critically acclaimed films in the 1990s with positive portrayals of American and world historical events. In 1993, he released *Schindler's List,* a fictionalized account of a real-life incident that occurred in Germany during World War II (1939–45). An opportunistic, amoral German businessman named Oskar Schindler has a change of heart, saving thousands of Jewish slave laborers at his factory from extermination by the Nazis. Many critics claimed the grainy black-and-white movie was the best film of the decade. Spielberg later returned to the World War II theme with *Saving Private Ryan* (1998). The film paid tribute to American soldiers who fought and died in the pivotal D-Day invasion of the beaches of Normandy, France, in June 1944.

❖ TALK RADIO: FROM CONSERVATIVES TO SHOCK JOCKS

Throughout the last few decades of the twentieth century, conservative politicians, religious leaders, and other public figures often claimed that the American media (newspapers, television, radio) were controlled by liberals. (Conservatives, usually members of the Republican Party, favor preserving traditional values and customs. They oppose any sudden shift in the balance of power, and they believe that the federal government should have limited control over and involvement in the lives of average Americans. On the other hand, liberals, often belonging to the Democratic Party, favor a stronger central government. They support political reforms that try to extend democracy and civil rights fairly to all citizens and distribute wealth more evenly.) In the 1990s however, despite their complaints about the liberal media, conservatives found themselves in control of one particular medium: talk radio.

By the middle of the decade, talk radio had become the second most common radio format in the nation after country music. The number of talk stations exploded to one thousand, up from two hundred only ten years before. Many media critics believed most conservative radio talk-show hosts became popular because they were not afraid to offend people; they attacked topics as varied as feminism, welfare, gun control, and the president of the United States.

The most popular conservative radio talk-show host of the 1990s was Rush Limbaugh, whose three-hour show was heard daily by twenty million listeners. His derogatory on-air comments frequently targeted women, the poor, and minorities. Limbaugh's willingness to criticize liberals, sometimes completely disregarding the facts, nevertheless earned him a devoted following, who agreed with his views. Many of his loyal listeners were white, working-class males who felt threatened by increasing economic and social empowerment of women and minorities. Limbaugh's inflammatory comments angered organizations such as the National Organization for Women (NOW) and Fairness and Accuracy in Reporting (FAIR). After he constantly attacked feminists, referring to them as "femi-Nazis," NOW began a campaign to encourage advertisers to pull their spots from his show. FAIR released a report documenting the misinformation in many of Limbaugh's comments. For example, he contended that volcanoes did more to harm the protective ozone layer in Earth's atmosphere than human-produced chemicals, contrary to the views of hundreds of scientists around the world.

Another talk-show host who shared Limbaugh's views of feminism and the women's movement was Laura Schlessinger. Her three-hour daily radio talk show drew twenty million listeners, making her the second most popular talk-show host during the decade. Schlessinger, who had earned a doctorate degree in physiology and a license in marriage and family therapy, offered blunt advice to callers from all over the nation. Like Limbaugh's, many of Schlessinger's views were offensive to some people, especially her belief that women were not oppressed in modern American society.

The third leading radio host of the 1990s was the self-proclaimed "King of All Media," Howard Stern. Foul-mouthed and offensive, he was the best-known of the so-called "shock jocks." For using indecent and sexually graphic speech on the air, Stern was fined more than two million dollars during the decade by the Federal Communications Commission (FCC). A 1997 Gallup Poll found that although 90 percent of Americans had heard of Stern, 75 percent of those polled held an unfavorable opinion of him—especially women, older people, and college graduates. In 1998, Stern began hosting a nightly television show on E! Entertainment Television, which carried an MA (mature audiences) rating for its lewd content. Critics almost universally denounced the show, calling it a new low in television trash

The radio talk shows of the 1990s relied more on passion than substance. Though widely popular, conservative hosts seemed more concerned with attracting a loyal audience than discussing real issues. The tone of their shows was often mean-spirited and sometimes downright vicious. Nonetheless, talk radio seemed to provide a forum for some Americans to have their say—or at least to have someone say it for them.

Conservative talk show host Rush Limbaugh.
Reproduced by permission of AP/Wide World Photos.

❖ SHOCKUMENTARY: TV TALK SHOWS AND REALITY TV

Howard Stern's shocking behavior on his radio talk show was rivaled by participants on 1990s daytime television talk shows. Guests voluntarily appeared on these shows to air grievances, reveal secrets, or reunite with mysterious people from their pasts. According to many talk show guests, producers often tried to whip them into an emotional frenzy before they went on the air. The resulting dramatic outbursts proved entertaining for audiences and increased ratings for hosts such as Ricki Lake and Jerry Springer. For some, the tactic had deadly results: A guest on *Jenny Jones* who revealed his secret same-sex crush on another male on the show was later murdered by that man.

As the 1990s began, longtime talk-show host Phil Donahue led in the ratings, followed closely by Geraldo Rivera, Sally Jesse Raphael, and

Cameras in the Courtrooms

In the 1990s, the American appetite for "real" television grew. In addition to watching the many "shockumentaries" that broadcast everything from police chases to animal attacks, Americans began to tune in to courtroom television. Two types experienced increasing popularity throughout the decade: televised coverage of criminal trials and shows starring theatrical judges who generally heard civil cases.

In 1981, the U.S. Supreme Court ruled that television camera crews could film a criminal trial providing they did not violate the defendant's rights. Following that ruling, courtrooms across the nation began to welcome television cameras. By the 1990s, almost every state allowed them into some judicial proceedings and about two-thirds freely allowed them into trial courts at the judge's discretion.

The 1995 O. J. Simpson case, however, led to a rethinking of the impact of courtroom cameras. Simpson, the former football star, was charged with murdering his former wife Nicole Brown Simpson and her friend Ronald Goldman. Several news networks, including CNN, broadcast the murder trial live. Legal experts thought Judge Lance Ito did not handle his court-

Oprah Winfrey. Donahue and Winfrey, in particular, promoted shows dealing with information and interpersonal relationships, encouraging viewers to improve themselves. Winfrey went even further, focusing on personal empowerment, social activism, and book discussions.

All of that changed quickly in the early 1990s when the number of talk shows multiplied greatly. When hosts such as Maury Povich, Montel Williams, and Jenny Jones hit the airwaves in 1991, Jerry Springer in 1992, and Leeza Gibbons and Ricki Lake in 1993, trash TV emerged to dominate daytime television. While the earlier talk shows had not shied away from controversy, these newcomers added an element of confrontation, and suddenly screaming matches and fistfights became commonplace. With topics such as "Woman in love with a serial killer" and "Girlfriend, I slept with your man and I'll do it again," these shows played to whooping, cheering audiences. Along with the hosts and producers, the studio audiences encouraged the guests to sling mud at each other, with

room very well, and the cameras allowed the world to view the spectacle. Following the not-guilty verdict, many people blamed television coverage for influencing the trial's outcome, and many judges began to reconsider allowing cameras in their courtrooms.

Because of access to many courtrooms and rising public interest in the American judicial system, Steven Brill launched the Courtroom Television Network (Court TV) in July 1991. Highly successful from its inception, Court TV aired several high-profile cases during the decade, including the 1994 trial of Lyle and Erik Menendez, two Beverly Hills brothers accused of murdering their parents.

Real-life television courtroom trials began with *Divorce Court,* which ran from 1957 to 1969 and again from 1986 to 1991. Its popularity was eclipsed by Judge Joseph A. Wapner's *The People's Court,* which aired from 1981 to 1993. Following Wapner's success, other court shows took to the air. Judge Judy Sheindlin, Judge Joe Brown, Judge Greg Mathis, and Judge Mills Lane all handed out justice on their own daytime programs.

tempers flaring. In fact, the confrontation format was so successful that in February 1998 the *Jerry Springer* show nudged *Oprah* out of the number-one slot for the first time since 1987.

Quite often, talk-show producers' recruiting practices could be somewhat deceptive; many guests left the shows feeling they had been set up to be humiliated. In March 1995, producers invited Jonathon Schmitz to appear on the *Jenny Jones* show to meet a secret admirer. They chose not to tell Schmitz that his secret admirer was a man. Fellow guest Scott Amedure revealed his secret crush on Schmitz on national television. Three days after the show was videotaped, an angry and mortified Schmitz went to Amedure's home and killed him with two shotgun blasts.

Attempts to reform daytime television began soon after this tragic event. The *Rosie O'Donnell Show,* which debuted in June 1996, was the first of several new more wholesome, less confrontational talk shows. In 1997, journalist Barbara Walters launched *The View,* a daytime show hosted by a group

Top Television Shows of the 1990s

Year	Show
1990	Cheers
1991	60 Minutes
1992	60 Minutes
1993	60 Minutes
1994	Seinfeld
1995	ER
1996	ER
1997	Seinfeld
1998	ER
1999	Who Wants to Be a Millionaire

of women discussing everyday issues. The impact of these and other shows was widely felt in the industry. Geraldo Rivera cleaned up his act and left his talk show in 1998, moving on to NBC News. Even Springer agreed to eliminate his show's foul language and fistfights. His ratings then promptly slipped 17 percent, allowing *Oprah* to regain the number-one spot.

While daytime television was cleaning up its act, the ratings winners on 1990s evening television were "shockumentaries," a form of reality-based television showcasing shocking, violent, and gory footage of everything from police shootouts to unbelievably large tumors to natural disasters. They were inexpensive to produce and drew large numbers of viewers.

The shockumentary trend began in 1995 when the Columbia Broadcasting System (CBS) aired *World's Most Dangerous Animals,* but the Fox network perfected this brand of television show with *When Animals Attack.* In fact, the second installation of this show was so successful that Fox ran it twice during the November 1996 rating sweeps period (a period during which the networks measure ratings to determine future advertising rates).

One of the most successful reality-based programs, first aired in 1989, had broadcast more than four hundred episodes by the end of 1999. *COPS,* shown on Fox, showed real-life law enforcement officers chasing suspects, intervening in domestic disputes, and apprehending alleged murderers.

With ever-increasing violence shown television in the 1990s, parents and politicians became concerned about children's access to violent programming. As early as 1992, the technical standards for a "violence chip" (V-Chip), which could provide parents with a way to block particular television programs, were discussed at meetings of the Electronic Industries Association.

Included in the electronics of a television, the V-Chip reads information encoded in a rated program and blocks programs based on a parent's selections. In 1992, broadcasters vetoed the V-Chip, afraid it might limit audiences and advertising revenue. Two years later, however, the industry group agreed to begin including the device in more expensive televisions.

The U.S. Congress and President Bill Clinton recognized the need to provide parents with technology to help them control programming in their homes. In 1996, Congress passed and the president signed the Telecommunications Reform Act. Among other things, the act called for a V-Chip to be installed in every new television set. In response to this legislation, the television industry in 1997 submitted a voluntary system of parental guidelines for rating television programs to the Federal Communications Commission (FCC) for review. In March 1998, the FCC approved the rating system and adopted technical requirements for the V-Chip.

According to the FCC's requirements, all television sets with picture screens thirteen inches or larger must be equipped with the V-Chip. Half of all televisions manufactured after July 1, 1999, were required to carry the V-Chip, and all thirteen-inch or larger sets made after January 1, 2000, had to meet this requirement.

The show was nominated for four Emmy awards and won its time slot during the 1998 May sweeps. At the end of the decade, *COPS* was one of the longest-running programs on television, joining the ranks of the television newsmagazines *60 Minutes*, *20/20*, and *48 Hours*.

While *COPS* was an innovator in reality-based television, its images of police experiences were mild compared to the shock specials popular in the middle of the decade. Shows with titles such as *World's Deadliest Swarms, When Stunts Go Bad, Cheating Death: Catastrophes Caught on Tape,* and *World's Scariest Police Shootouts,* featured extremely violent and gory content. Some television critics chided the networks for televising such shows, but others believed the specials depicted the same violence shown every day on local news programs. Despite the debate, shockumentaries continued to be highly successful at the close of the 1990s.

❖ LITERATURE: READING GROUPS AND SUPERSTARS

Though critics bemoaned the declining quality of books, reading became more popular in the 1990s than it had been in decades. By 1999, there were approximately five hundred thousand readers' book clubs in the United States, nearly double the number that existed in 1994. The book club formed in 1996 by popular daytime television talk-show host Oprah Winfrey accelerated the trend, but the popularity of book clubs had begun to soar even earlier.

Meeting in libraries, bookstores, and private homes, book clubs attracted readers of all ages and in all regions of the country, appealing to a wide variety of literary tastes. Some were devoted to mysteries or romances; others focused on classic or contemporary fiction, biography, science fiction, history, or books dealing with social issues. Children's reading groups became especially popular. A survey conducted by *Publishers' Weekly* magazine in 1998 indicated that 78 percent of teenagers thought reading was a "cool thing to do," while 86 percent said that they read "for fun." Sixty percent of teenagers who read on a regular basis believed that they were smarter than their peers who did not. People also joined reading clubs for reasons other than their love of books. For many, membership in a reading club provided an opportunity to discuss something besides work and family and to express their ideas to others.

When Oprah Winfrey started a book club, no one, perhaps not even Winfrey, expected her book selections to influence book buyers. But viewers trusted her choices, and Oprah's Book Club became a national phenomenon. Books she recommended became immediate best-sellers. She transformed unknown writers into national names and introduced well-known authors to whole new audiences. A recommendation by Winfrey meant that book would sell hundreds of thousands of copies. In December 1996, after Winfrey selected Toni Morrison's 1977 novel, *Song of Solomon,* as the second book-club offering, one million copies of the novel were sold. In fact, Morrison experienced more commercial success as a result of Winfrey's selection than she had after she won the Nobel Prize in Literature in 1993.

In choosing books by new writers as well as by established ones, Winfrey was guided by her own tastes. Her wide-ranging selections included

Toni Morrison and the Nobel Prize

Over her long career as a writer, Toni Morrison has used poetic language in an unflinching examination of gender conflicts, race relations, and other aspects of American society. When she won the Nobel Prize for Literature in 1993, she became the first American woman to receive the prestigious award since Pearl Buck in 1938. Perhaps more noteworthy, she became the first African American woman ever to be so honored.

The Nobel Foundation is a private institution founded in 1900 based on the last will and testament of Swedish inventor and philanthropist Alfred Nobel (1833–1896). Each year since then, the foundation has given awards—the Nobel Prizes—to individuals for their accomplishments in the fields of chemistry, literature, peace, physics, and physiology or medicine. In 1969, the foundation added an award in the field of economics.

Generally, the foundation awards the Nobel Prize for Literature to a writer whose body of work merits attention. In doing so, the foundation may cite one or more of the writer's works that are especially outstanding.

In its press release announcing the awarding of a Nobel Prize to Morrison, the foundation stated that "Morrison is a literary artist of the first rank.

She delves into the language itself, a language she wants to liberate from the fetters of race. And she addresses us with the lustre of poetry." In particular, the foundation cited Morrison's *Song of Solomon* (1977), a complex study of black family life and the search for love and meaning in family history, and *Beloved* (1987), a mesmerizing story about the legacy of slavery. *Photo reproduced by permission of Chris Felver.*

novels that dealt with disabled children, missing persons, bitter divorces, the ties that bind in a black community, and responsibility in the death of a child. Some critics denounced the selections as sentimental, unnecessarily graphic, or sexist. For members of her book club, however, Winfrey's taste in reading material was on the mark: It resembled their own.

Best-selling Fiction of the 1990s

Year	Title	Author
1990	*The Plains of Passage*	Jean M. Auel
1991	*Scarlett: The Sequel to Margaret Mitchell's "Gone With the Wind"*	Alexandra Ripley
1992	*Dolores Claiborne*	Stephen King
1993	*The Bridges of Madison County*	Robert James Waller
1994	*The Chamber*	John Grisham
1995	*The Rainmaker*	John Grisham
1996	*The Runaway Jury*	John Grisham
1997	*The Partner*	John Grisham
1998	*The Street Lawyer*	John Grisham
1999	*The Testament*	John Grisham

The general literary taste of the American public created a few publishing superstars in the 1990s. Horror-fiction writer Stephen King, a one-man best-seller factory throughout the 1980s, continued to turn out hits at the beginning of the 1990s. However, he was soon eclipsed at the top of the charts by lawyer-turned-novelist John Grisham, who transformed the legal thriller into a best-selling phenomenon. Beginning in mid-decade, he dominated the publishing world. His books spent unprecedented weeks—and months—on best-seller lists, numbered more than sixty million copies in print across the world, and were translated into thirty-one languages. A number of his works in the decade also were adapted into popular films.

Another publishing phenomenon in the 1990s was *The Bridges of Madison County*. Written over a two-week period by Robert James Waller, the novel focused on the fateful union of Robert Kincaid, a free-spirited, wandering photographer, and Francesca Johnson, a war bride living on an Iowa farm far from her native Italy. Literary critics panned the 1992 book but American public loved it. It remained on the best-seller lists for well over a year and broke many sales records. In 1995, the novel was adapted into a Steven Spielberg film starring Meryl Streep and Clint Eastwood.

During 1999, thousands of young children proudly displayed tattoos in the shape of a purple lightning bolt on their foreheads. Many adults were puzzled. For those in the know, however, the temporary tattoos indicated that these kids were fans of the young, wizard-in-training Harry Potter. The fictional character and his magical adventures, the creation of English author J. K. Rowling, captivated readers young and old.

Three books, *Harry Potter and the Sorcerer's Stone* (1998), *Harry Potter and the Chamber of Secrets* (1999), and *Harry Potter and the Prisoner of Azkaban* (1999), racked up record-breaking sales in the United Kingdom and the United States. The books also earned the distinction as one of the few children's books ever to crack the adult best-sellers list, remaining on the *New York Times* best- sellers' list for more than thirty-eight weeks.

By the fall of 1999, more than 7.5 million volumes were in print, translated into twenty-eight languages, with more than 650,000 lightning-bolt tattoos also being sold at local bookstores across the country.

As the next decade and new century began, Rowling continued to publish further adventures of Harry Potter, and the frenzy over the novels continued. In 2001, a film adaptation of the first novel was released, bringing the Harry Potter sensation to movie screens worldwide.

❖ GRUNGE, GANSTA RAP, A LATINO RESURGENCE, AND A DIVA FOR THE DECADE

A new form of rock music—grunge—arose in the 1990s, combining elements of punk rock and heavy metal. Characterized by distorted guitar sounds and lyrics of despair, grunge emerged from the Seattle, Washington, music scene where it had been popular for most of the 1980s. Grunge musicians thought of themselves as authentic street rockers, not as a bunch of packaged bands hyped by prominent producers. The bands that succeeded, however, did so because they signed contracts with major record labels, leaving behind other local talent.

The record company most responsible for introducing grunge to a national audience was Seattle-based Sub Pop Records, which signed bands such as Green River, Soundgarden, Blood Circus, Swallow, Nirvana, and

Members of the band Nirvana (left to right, Chris Novoselic, Dave Grohl, and Kurt Cobain) in 1991. *Reproduced by permission of AP/Wide World Photos.*

TAD. These bands, along with Mudhoney, Alice in Chains, Screaming Trees, and Pearl Jam, quickly brought a much-needed end to the tired, dated sound of mainstream rock that had dominated the 1980s.

The best-known of the grunge bands was Nirvana, formed in 1986 in Olympia, Washington, by Kurt Cobain and Kris Novoselic, who had played together in other groups. In 1988, they signed a record deal with Sub Pop Records and released the single "Love Buzz." The band's first album, *Bleach,* was released in the following year. It was unpolished, but Cobain was already demonstrating his melodic and lyrical creativity. By 1991 Nirvana had parted company with Sub Pop and signed with Geffen, through which the band released its second album, *Nevermind.* From the moment the first copies of the first single from the album, "Smells Like Teen Spirit," went out to radio, the excitement started growing. By the time the first reviews of *Nevermind* appeared in the music press, Nirvana was already on its way. Three months after its release, the album reached number one.

Soon after, the band performed on *Saturday Night Live* and recorded an acoustic session for the MTV *Unplugged* series. In 1993, Nirvana released *In Utero,* which many critics thought was an even stronger record than *Nevermind.* Despite such success, Kurt Cobain was consumed by an addiction to heroin. He nearly overdosed on a sedative in Rome in early 1994, and in April of that year, he shot and killed himself in his garage. His death ended the life of Nirvana as well. The other band members dissolved Nirvana and later formed separate musical groups.

In the 1980s, rap music had emerged as one of the most original new music forms, with artists such as Run-DMC and LL Cool J spreading the Bronx-born sound from Brooklyn to Beverly Hills. Yet few would have expected performers such as MC Hammer and Vanilla Ice to make rap music a force in pop radio. By the 1990s, rap's authentic voice of urban youth had evolved into mindless jingles with polished beats played at suburban school dances nationwide. Rap had left the ghetto and lost touch with its roots.

At the beginning of the decade, some performers decided to take rap back to the streets. Street credibility became an essential part of rap music. Taking their cues from early hard-core artists such as Public Enemy and Boogie Down Productions, West Coast artists such as former N.W.A. members Dr. Dre and Ice Cube tried to convey the violence of living in the ghetto through a new style called gangsta rap. It became the predominant sound of the early 1990s. The more menacing it sounded, with references to guns and illegal substances, the better it was received by a naive, largely white, suburban teenage audience. In 1993, Snoop Doggy Dogg's *Doggystyle* became the first debut album ever to enter the pop-album chart at number one.

At the same time gangsta rap arose in the West, another hip-hop sound was emerging on the East Coast. New, positive-minded groups started to bring a jazzier style to rap music. Groups such as the Jungle Brothers, A Tribe Called Quest, De La Soul, and Leaders of the New School formed a new alliance called the Native Tongues, which focused on black thought and black history. Alongside other influential groups, such as EPMD and Gang Starr, their soulful sounds and creative rhymes brought the hip-hop culture back to the music.

During the last half of the decade, people who were concerned with preserving the roots of hip-hop culture began to call themselves hip-hop artists to distinguish themselves from rappers. A divide that had developed between East Coast and West Coast groups earlier in the decade grew stronger. Some

Rap artist Snoop Doggy Dogg performing on stage at the Shrine Auditorium in Los Angeles. **Reproduced by permission of AP/Wide World Photos.**

claim the conflicts between the two groups were responsible for the murders of two superstars: Tupac Shakur in 1996 and Notorious B.I.G. in 1997. By the end of the decade, hip-hop had splintered even further.

Another musical style popular in the 1990s was the Latin sound, and one reason for its renewed popularity was Ricky Martin. Formerly one of the teen vocalists in the popular 1980s Latin group Menudo, Martin made the most of his handsome Latin looks and his considerable vocal talents during

Top Singles of the 1990s

Year	Song	Artist
1990	"Hold On"	Wilson Phillips
1991	"(Everything I Do) I Do It for You"	Bryan Adams
1992	"End of the Road"	Boyz II Men
1993	"I Will Always Love You"	Whitney Houston
1994	"The Sign"	Ace of Base
1995	"Gansta's Paradise"	Coolio featuring L.V.
1996	"Macarena"	Los Del Rio
1997	"Something About the Way You Look Tonight/Candle in the Wind '97"	Elton John
1998	"Too Close"	Next
1999	"Believe"	Cher

the late 1990s. In February 1999, Martin impressed the audience at the Grammy Awards show with an electrifying performance of his worldwide smash hit, "La Copa de la Vida" ("The Cup of Life"). Later that year, his first English-language album, *Ricky Martin,* hit number one on the album charts. "Livin' La Vida Loca," the debut single from the album, became the biggest-selling number-one single in the history of Columbia Records.

One other Latin artist who gained broad appeal during the 1990s was Jennifer Lopez. A dancer, actress, and singer, Lopez was thrust into the spotlight in 1997 for her film portrayal of murdered Tejano singing sensation Selena. Other film roles showcasing her talents quickly followed. In the summer of 1999, Lopez released her first album, *On the 6.* The first single, "If You Had My Love," topped the music charts for five weeks.

Perhaps the most prolific singer-songwriter of the 1990s was Mariah Carey. Her debut album, *Mariah Carey,* was released by Columbia Records in 1990. Despite its syrupy-sweet lyrics, it sold six million copies, and two songs from the album reached number one on the charts. She won two Grammy awards in 1991, one for Best Pop Vocal Performance and another for Best New Artist.

Carey, who had been writing songs by the time she was in high school, soon became involved in the entire process of creating her subsequent albums, from writing or cowriting the songs to arranging and coproducing. Only five of the singles she released during the decade failed to reach number one on the pop charts. She had more number-one hits than any other female soloist, and only eight fewer number-one hits than Elvis Presley, the all-time leader. A perfectionist, Carey once recorded one hundred versions of the same song ("Honey").

For More Information

BOOKS

Cross, Charles R. *Heavier Than Heaven: A Biography of Kurt Cobain.* New York: Hyperion, 2001.

Dyson, Michael Eric. *Holler If You Hear Me: Searching for Tupac Shakur.* New York: Basic Books, 2001.

Johns, Michael-Anne, and Catherine Murphy. *Jennifer Lopez.* Kansas City, MO: Andrews McMeel Publishing, 2000.

Kramer, Barbara. *Toni Morrison: Nobel Prize-Winning Author.* Berkeley Heights, NJ: Enslow Publishers, 1996.

Krohn, Katherine. *Oprah Winfrey.* Minneapolis, MN: Lerner Publications, 2001.

Weaver, Robyn M. *John Grisham.* San Diego, CA: Lucent Books, 1999.

WEB SITES

The Grammy Awards. http://www.infoplease.com/ipa/A0150533.html (accessed on May 1, 2002).

National Endowment for the Arts. http://arts.endow.gov/ (accessed on May 1, 2002).

V-Chip Education Project. http://www.vchipeducation.org/ (accessed on May 1, 2002).

Welcome to in the 90s: The Nineties Nostalgia Site. http://www.inthe90s.com/index.shtml (accessed on May 1, 2002).

Yesterdayland—Pop Music in the 90s. http://www.yesterdayland.com/popopedia/shows/decades/music_1990s.php (accessed on May 1, 2002).

chapter two *Business and the Economy*

1990: **January 10** Warner Brothers Communications and Time Inc. complete a $14.1 billion merger, establishing the largest media conglomerate in the world.

1990: **April 12** Under pressure from environmental groups, three top U.S. canneries implement "dolphin-safe" tuna-catching practices.

1990: **June 4** Greyhound Lines Inc., the bus company, files for bankruptcy.

1991: **January 8** Pan American World Airways (Pam Am) files for bankruptcy.

1991: **April 7** The Dow Jones Industrial Average closes above 3,000 points for the first time.

1991: **July 3** Apple Computer and IBM publicly join together in an effort to exchange technologies and develop new equipment.

1992: General Motors announces a record $4.5 billion loss in 1991 and says it will close twenty-one plants and lay off some seventy-four thousand workers in the next four years.

1992: **April 23** McDonald's opens its first fast-food restaurant in Beijing, China.

1992: **June 5** The federal government announces that the unemployment rate has jumped to 7.5 percent, the highest level in nearly eight years.

1993: **February 4** A jury finds General Motors guilty of negligence; the company knew of a faulty fuel-tank design that caused the death of a teenager but did nothing about it. The jury awards $105.2 million to the teenager's parents.

1993: **June 8** The Equal Employment Opportunity Commission (EEOC) rules that employers cannot refuse to hire disabled employees because of high insurance costs.

1994: **January 1** The North American Free Trade Agreement (NAFTA) goes into effect.

1994: **April 4** Netscape Communications is founded.

1994: **July 15** In a settlement with the U.S. Justice Department, Microsoft promises to end monopolistic practices it used to dominate the personal computer software market.

1995: **February 14** A federal judge rejects the U.S. Justice Department's proposed antitrust settlement with Microsoft and orders the company to be broken up; the decision is later overturned on appeal.

1995: **February 26** The United States and China avert a trade war by signing an agreement to reduce trade barriers between the two countries.

1995: **November 21** The Dow Jones Industrial Average closes above the 5,000 mark for the first time, rising 40.46 points to 5,023.55

1996: For the first time, personal-computer sales exceed the sale of television sets.

1996: **September 6** The jobless rate is reported at 5.1 percent, the lowest figure in seven years.

1996: **November 15** Texaco settles for a record $140 million a racial discrimination lawsuit brought by some of its employees. Executives had taped their disparaging remarks about minorities and their plans to destroy incriminating evidence; the tapes prompted the monetary out-of-court settlement.

1997: **January 9** Volkswagen agrees to pay one hundred million dollars to General Motors to settle an espionage lawsuit in which a former GM executive was accused of stealing trade secrets when he moved to the German automaker.

1997: **January 31** The federal government reports that the rate of inflation has sunk to its lowest level in thirty years.

1997: **September 1** The minimum wage is raised from $4.75 to $5.15 an hour—the last time it will be raised in the decade.

1998: With a market value of over $260 billion, Microsoft passes General Electric as the biggest company in the United States.

1998: **May 14** Just hours before state and federal governments are set to file extensive antitrust lawsuits against Microsoft, the company agrees to postpone the launch of its newest operating system, Windows 98 for three days.

1998: **December 1** The largest U.S. oil company, Exxon, announces it will buy the second-largest oil company, Mobil, for eighty billion dollars, forming the largest corporation in the world.

1999: **May 3** The Dow Jones Industrial Average closes at about 11,000 only twenty-four trading days after breaking the 10,000 mark, making it the fastest stock market rise in history.

1999: **September 7** Viacom Inc. announces it will buy the CBS Corporation for $37.3 billion, making it the largest media merger ever. The new conglomerate becomes the second-largest media company in the world (after Time Warner).

✳ *Overview* . . . .

The remarkable performance of the U.S. economy in the 1990s called into question many long-standing economic assumptions, practices, and values. Suddenly, and in many instances quite unexpectedly, the old rules governing business seemed to have become obsolete. No one knew for sure what the new rules were going to be. A unpredictable decade for business, it was as full of opportunity as of peril.

This upheaval resulted primarily from the arrival of the Internet, which transformed life for most Americans. Suddenly, the whole world was more accessible, as an unprecedented quantity and variety of information enabled companies and individuals to function more efficiently and profitably. The Internet fundamentally changed business as brash, computer-savvy entrepreneurs overshadowed many of their counterparts who found themselves struggling to make sense of the new cyberworld.

Internet technology may also have permanently enhanced the economy and accelerated its rate of growth, while keeping at bay the inflation of prices and wages that in the past had undermined prosperity. Companies merged to form bigger, richer, and more powerful entities. Experts speculated about how long the boom could last and what, if anything, might finally bring it to an end. No one, though, could deny that a new economy began to take shape, one that differed substantially from what economists had expected. The most startling aspect of this new economy was that it challenged the view that inflation would inevitably result from a growth rate higher than 2.5 percent coupled with an unemployment rate below 5 percent. In the 1990s, both of these conditions were met, yet the economy continued to prosper.

The "new economy" affected different sectors of the workforce in various ways. The top few workers received high salaries, in part because often there were not enough individuals with the specialized skills needed to fill these positions. Women and minorities made gains in the workplace but, on the whole, they were still denied access to the top business positions. In response, many women in the decade left the corporate world and started their own small businesses.

Multinational corporations increasingly dominated the world economy during the 1990s, pushing forward economic globalization. Eight corporations, seven of them American, were among the top twenty-five economic entities in the world. As the decade drew to a close, Americans living in a digital economy prepared to enter an economic future of electronic money and mammoth financial and business conglomerates.

Jeff Bezos (1964–) Jeff Bezos had a vision that the Internet would revolutionize commerce. And he had one simple ambition: to own and operate the biggest store on Earth. To that end, on July 16, 1995, Bezos launched Amazon.com, the world's largest online bookstore. Within a few years, the Web site began offering music CDs, videos, toys, tools, and electronics, among other items. Although the company lost money every year it operated during the 1990s, the number of customers visiting the company's site increased yearly. In 1999, Amazon had sales approaching $1 billion. *Photo reproduced by permission of Amazon.com Inc.*

Ken Chenault (1951–) Ken Chenault became senior card executive of American Express, the credit card company, in 1991. He quickly led a cost-cutting overhaul of the company, and in 1995 was promoted to vice chairman. Finally, in late 1999, the Chief Executive Officer (CEO) of American Express, Harvey Golub, announced Chenault would become the company's new CEO by 2001. Although he was not the first African American to be named a CEO, he was the first to control a global financial services company. *Photo reproduced by permission of Timothy Greenfield-Sanders.*

Bill Gates (1955–) Bill Gates led the Microsoft Corporation as it grew rapidly through the 1980s and 1990s to become the wealthiest company and the tenth-largest economic entity in the world. As of 1999, the computer software giant had a market value of $546 billion. At the same time, Gates had amassed personal wealth of $87.5 billion. He also started philanthropic foundations to support charitable measures in global public health and education. In the late 1990s, the federal government took Microsoft to court, claiming the company was a monopoly and needed to be divided into several small companies to comply with federal antitrust laws. *Photo reproduced by permission of AP/Wide World Photos.*

Alan Greenspan (1926–) Alan Greenspan served throughout the 1990s as chairman of the Federal Reserve Board, which sets interest rates, controls the money supply, and oversees the economic health of the country. Although some business leaders thought his tight monetary policies kept business profits down, others praised his handling of interest rates that helped stabilize the economy. Toward the end of the decade, Greenspan proved more willing to allow the economy to grow without raising interest rates to stem inflation (the continuing rise in the general price of goods because of an overabundance of available money). *Photo reproduced by permission of Archive Photos, Inc.*

❖ THE INTERNET AND BIG BUSINESS

In October 1969, two teams of computer scientists, one at the University of California, Los Angeles, and the other at the Bell Laboratories in Menlo Park, California, linked computers over telephone lines to operate as a single system. The U.S. military had sponsored the research, seeking to establish a national communications network that would continue to operate even if part of the system were disabled or destroyed in a nuclear attack. Thus began the Internet Age.

During the 1990s, the Internet became a force that transformed every aspect of life. Anyone with a computer, telephone, and modem literally had at his or her fingertips a staggering quantity and variety of information. As the decade drew to a close, the possibilities of the new technology seemed endless.

The initial impact of the Internet has been profound, especially for business. Financial markets became more accessible and efficient for those who wished to raise or invest money. Accessibility and efficiency, in fact, defined the Internet. Upstart online companies humbled large corporations that had been dominant for decades. If online sales of industrial and consumer goods and services were combined with the equipment and software needed to operate and support e-commerce, the Internet economy totaled more than $300 billion in 1999. By comparison, the U.S. automobile industry was worth $350 billion that same year.

A host of new businesses emerged from the Internet during the decade: new companies, business models, corporate structures, terminology, even industries. Confusion reigned supreme. Experts could not agree on what was happening, or on what the future was likely to bring. In the early 1990s, the World Wide Web (a graphical user interface for the Internet) made the Internet easier for nonprogrammers to use, calling into question all the former truths about how to conduct business. In 1997, for instance, Yahoo! Inc. was nothing more than a Web search engine and directory. By 1999, it had become a multibillion-dollar major media company. Perhaps more amazing, companies such as Amazon.com and eToys Inc., which by the end of the decade had yet to turn a profit, continued to attract untold numbers of investors. These success stories certainly perplexed traditional business executives who had spent their working lives trying to build companies with bricks-and-mortar offices, factories, assets, and profits.

One inescapable fact of doing business in the 1990s was that the Internet put customers in charge as never before. With access to the wealth of information that the Internet provided, customers pointed and clicked their way to the best goods and services at the lowest prices. The Internet offered new advantages as well as to merchants, who could now identify individual customers and collect unprecedented quantities of data about the character and pattern of their purchases. Yet the rise of the Internet compelled executives to rethink the nature of the companies they managed. Suddenly, factories, stores, trucks, warehouses, and even employees, once regarded as assets, came to be seen as unnecessary costs and liabilities. Savvy companies began to eliminate, or to avoid altogether, building costly facilities or hiring legions of sales representatives. They concentrated instead on expanding their capacity to use the Internet.

Experts agreed that the single most important reason for the dramatic worldwide explosion in economic productivity and market value during the 1990s was the advent of the Internet. The Internet altered the dynamics of the global economy at least as much as the introduction of railroads and electricity had during the nineteenth century. The rise of the Internet has also meant that the traditional requirements of economic growth and development—access to and control of resources and labor—may no

*A packed Amazon.com
distribution warehouse at
Christmastime in 1999.
Reproduced by permission of
AP/Wide World Photos.*

Living through one of the biggest economic booms in U.S. history provided many Americans with the opportunity to amass great personal fortunes. Whether by getting lucky in the stock market, making the most of stock options, or being in on the ground floor of an Internet start-up, many Americans struck it rich in the 1990s. So many, in fact, that perseverance and perspiration seemed destined to fall by the wayside. Between 1995 and 1998, about one million new millionaires appeared. The phrase "having two commas" signified that someone had achieved his or her first million (in reference to the number of commas used when one million is represented numerically). The number of Americans "having three commas," or their first billion, went up, too. *Forbes* magazine reported in 1999 that on its list of the four hundred richest Americans, 250 were billionaires, up 60 from the previous year.

longer be the principal keys of economic strength. Economic power became increasingly linked to the control, accessibility, and manipulation of information.

By 1999, the United States dominated the Internet, accounting for more than 50 percent of all individuals online and 75 percent of all Internet commerce. Not surprisingly, the first country to develop and utilize Internet technology enjoyed the lion's share of the economic benefits it generated. Most experts predicted, however, that this advantage would decline over time as the number of European and Asian households with access to the Internet would increase dramatically early in the twenty-first century. In fact, by the end of the 1990s, Iceland, Finland, and Sweden already had more Internet users per capita than the United States.

❖ THE BOOMING "NEW ECONOMY"

The second half of the 1990s marked the longest sustained stretch of economic growth in U.S. history. Unlike other periods of long-term economic expansion, this one was not reversed by rising inflation (the continuing rise in the general price of goods and services because of an overabundance of available money). Growth during the decade continued and even accelerated as inflation declined. Rapid technological change, the rise of the services sector, and the emergence of the global marketplace all combined to keep the economy moving.

A new U.S. economy had begun to take shape, one that defied many long-standing principles. Normally in a period of economic expansion, the federal government spends more money than it takes in—a practice called deficit spending. Yet between 1992 and 1997, deficit spending decreased from $290 billion to $67 billion. Another economic theory debunked in the 1990s was the belief that a growth rate of 2.5 percent coupled with an unemployment rate below 5 percent was guaranteed to generate inflation. After 1993, however, the U.S. economy grew at an annual rate of about 4 percent, and by the second half of the decade unemployment fell below 5 percent for the first time since the 1970s. Yet inflation did not arise to slow down or reverse these economic advances.

The majority of economists attributed these developments to a restructuring of companies, the growth of the Internet and the high-technology industry, and governmental policies such as the 1994 North American Free Trade Agreement (NAFTA) between Canada, Mexico, and the United States. This accord established a free-trade zone in North America. Tariffs (duties or taxes placed on imported or exported goods by governments) were lifted on the majority of goods produced by the three nations. In turn, this helped create a continental economy without national borders that initiated and sustained economic development. NAFTA further allowed companies to relocate facilities and jobs to locations both inside and outside the United States where they could pay lower wages. In addition, these companies hired growing numbers of temporary workers to whom they provided no health or retirement benefits. Taken together, these procedures helped companies lower their costs while increasing their profits.

As the decade drew to a close, economists wondered about the course the U.S. economy would take in the twenty-first century. It became painfully evident that the old rules governing the economy no longer applied; but it was equally obvious that no one knew what the new rules would be. Economists speculated that traditional indicators such as inflation, monetary policy, or interest rates may not determine future economic growth; rather, a lack of preparation, planning, education, and skills may prevent U.S. business from taking full advantage of opportunities in the dynamic "new economy."

❖ CHANGING THE FACE OF BUSINESS

Throughout the 1990s, business offered women a mixture of advances and disappointments. Increasing numbers of women entered the workplace and moved into traditionally male-dominated occupations. At the

American Nobel Prize Winners in Economics

Year	Economist
1990	Harry M. Markowitz Merton H. Miller William F. Sharpe
1991	No award given to an American
1992	Gary S. Becker
1993	Robert W. Fogel Douglass C. North
1994	John C. Harsanyi John F. Nash Jr.
1995	Robert E. Lucas Jr.
1996	William Vickrey
1997	Robert C. Merton Myron S. Scholes
1998	No award given to an American
1999	No award given to an American

same time, women were paid on average 30 percent less than their male counterparts. The National Committee on Pay Equity found that women lost an average $12,573 per year, or as much as $440,047 during the course of a lifetime, because of unequal pay practices.

Although acknowledging how far they had come, women recognized how far they still had to go. While they experienced less overt discrimination, they continued to battle for acceptance and equality. Many women occupied middle management positions, but they did not rise to the upper levels of the corporate world in representative numbers. As a result of such limitations, as well as concerns about having the flexibility to balance home life and career, many women opted out of the corporate world altogether and went into business for themselves.

According to a 1998 survey conducted by the Office of Advocacy of the U.S. Small Business Administration, 8.5 million women owned businesses in the United States in 1997. That figure increased to 9.1 million by 1999, and accounted for more than 33 percent of all small businesses.

1995: Average Wages and Cost of Goods

Median household income	$34,076.00
Minimum wage	$4.25
Cost of an average new home	$158,700.00
Cost of a gallon of regular gas	$1.15
Cost of a first-class stamp	$0.32
Cost of a gallon of milk	$2.96
Cost of a dozen eggs	$1.16
Cost of a loaf of bread	$1.23

Between 1992 and 1999, the number of women-owned businesses in each of the top fifty metropolitan areas in the country grew from between 33 and 50 percent, generating a combined $2.1 trillion in annual sales.

Like white women, minorities continued to make some progress in corporate America during the 1990s. Native Americans, African Americans, Asian Americans, Hispanic Americans, and members of other minority groups advanced to positions of prominence, authority, and high salaries with greater frequency than ever before. These gains notwithstanding, business experts agreed that minorities were still underrepresented at the highest levels of corporate management.

Although the U.S. population includes approximately 30 percent minorities, statistics for the decade showed fewer minorities entering upper management or sitting on the boards of directors of public corporations. Although the prosperous economy of the 1990s had increased wages and employment opportunities for nearly all workers, the benefits of that prosperity were not shared equally. This inequity was evident even among minorities who attained a level of education comparable with their white counterparts. Statistics compiled by the federal government in 1997 revealed that a white male college graduate earned a median wage of $21.45 per hour. An Asian male with the same degree earned $19.86 per hour. Similarly educated Hispanic and African American males made $17.37 and $16.53, respectively.

In the 1990s, executives who were more than fifty years of age became an endangered species in the corporate world. Riding the downsizing

Pets at Work

One trend that became popular at several companies during the 1990s was the practice of allowing people to bring their pets to work. Netscape Communications began the practice when it introduced an office policy, Dogs At Work. Eventually, not only dogs were invited to visit their master's office but also cats and even fish.

The rules were simple: A pet could stay as long as it behaved and did not break the two incidents rule (dirtying the carpet, fighting with other pets, biting the boss). Once a pet violated that rule, it could not come back until it had graduated from obedience training. Netscape and other companies that had similar policies found that, in many cases, worker productivity went up because workers' stress was reduced. Another benefit was that people were willing to work longer hours if they did not have to worry about their pets at home.

Citing health and safety concerns, some companies refused to adopt such pet-friendly policies. Other employers, such as Ben and Jerry's Ice Cream, offered a compromise: employees were allowed to bring their pets to work for the annual Dog Days of Summer party where the pet visitors were given a free flea dip and a lunch of hot dogs.

wave, companies could not get rid of them quickly enough. Then something curious happened. Companies began to face a crisis: those executives who opted for, or who were compelled to accept, early retirement left many companies facing a shortage of managerial talent. No one was left to train the next generation of business leaders.

As a consequence, many corporations sought to retain their most talented and experienced executives. Some of these companies fashioned consulting contracts and part-time assignments to accommodate older workers. Others went so far as to bring older workers out of retirement to provide stability and experience in critical positions and to pass on their knowledge, wisdom, and skills to younger colleagues.

❖ GLOBALIZATION: THE ECONOMY IN A BORDERLESS WORLD

The power and influence of multinational corporations grew during the 1990s, so much so that these companies rather than their host nations drove globalization—a new global economy unencumbered by national borders.

In 1999, the United States government dominated the world with a market value (the total value of goods and services produced that can be sold on the open market) in U.S. dollars of $15.013 trillion. Japan was a distant second, followed by the United Kingdom, France, and Germany. But eight of the top twenty-five economic entities in the world were corporations. Of the eight companies on the list, seven were American, and the top company was Microsoft, in tenth place with a market value of $546 billion. It ranked higher than countries such as Australia, Spain, Taiwan, and Sweden. The rest of the companies on the list were General Electric, Cisco Systems, Intel, Exxon-Mobil, Wal-Mart, Nippon, and AOL Time Warner.

Much of the economic power formerly controlled by nations also now resided in such international institutions as the European Union (EU), the World Trade Organization (WTO), and the International Monetary Fund (IMF). These entities gained substantial control over the national economies of many countries during the 1990s.

Critics of this development pointed out that nations would lose the strength of their individual governments to a world government that would form as a result of the concentration of power in multinational and international hands. Defenders of globalization, on the contrary, believed it was an inevitable change and the only question remaining was what sort of world economy and government would be established. Nations have always traded with one another for their mutual benefit, they argued

Those who backed globalization cited Mexico as an example of how a country can benefit from opening its markets to free trade and economic competition. The 1994 North American Free Trade Agreement (NAFTA) among Mexico, Canada, and the United States lifted tariffs (duties or taxes placed on imported or exported goods by governments) on most goods produced by the three nations. With no trade barriers, goods flowed freely among the nations. Politicians on both sides of the Mexican-U.S. border pointed out that the poorest Mexican cities have reaped the most benefits from NAFTA by gaining investments and high-wage manufacturing jobs.

Other international observers have disagreed. They argued that while Mexican workers may have moved from sugar cane farms and corn fields to factories, their wages and purchasing power actually declined. Those against globalization also pointed out that it favors developed countries and multinational corporations. Already the wealthiest nation, the United States gained the most from economic globalization. Perhaps most important, an international free market did not eliminate the economic differ-

The 1990s was of one of the most sustained periods of economic growth and prosperity in U.S. history. Yet, during the second half of the decade, the federal government paid out approximately $125 billion per year to corporations. Advocates applauded these payments as promoting economic development. Critics denounced them as corporate welfare.

Corporate welfare can be defined as any action by a local, state, or federal government that gives a corporation or an entire industry a benefit not offered to others. These advantages can come in many forms. Governments regularly extend significant tax breaks to corporations: permitting them to pay only a certain percent of their assessed property taxes, granting them the right to make purchases without paying sales tax, or reducing or eliminating taxes on their corporate profits. Corporate welfare also comes in the form of loans from cities and states at interest rates much lower than banks normally charge. In addition, governments often award grants to fund research that enables companies to improve productivity and enhance profits.

The justification for corporate welfare has long been that government should help companies create jobs. Yet, according to labor statistics, the companies in the 1990s that received the most corporate welfare eliminated more jobs than they created. During the same period, the U.S. Congress voted to reduce welfare payments to individuals and families, believing that welfare was unjust, destroyed the incentive to work, and created an economic dependence among those who received it.

The difference between corporations and individuals? Corporations have a lobby that is strong and powerful and that has access to government officials in city halls, statehouses, Capitol Hill, and the White House. Individuals do not.

ences between rich and poor countries. Nor did it resolve economic, social, and political inequalities within nations, as well as the crucial global problems of environmental standards and workers' rights.

Environmentalists, union organizers, and human-rights activists brought many of these issues and concerns to worldwide attention with the violent demonstrations that disrupted the meeting of the WTO held in

Seattle, Washington, in December 1999. Mindful of the problems that globalization created, economic, political, and corporate leaders began to address these issues as the decade closed, even if a way had not yet been found to solve them.

 For More Information

BOOKS

Lesinski, Jeanne M. *Bill Gates*. Minneapolis, MN: Lerner Publications, 2000.

McCormick, Anita Louise. *The Internet: Surfing the Issues*. Berkeley Heights, NJ: Enslow Publishers, 1998.

Spector, Robert. *Amazon.com: Get Big Fast*. New York: HarperBusiness, 2000.

WEB SITES

Board of Governors of the Federal Reserve System. http://www.federalreserve.gov/ (accessed on May 5, 2002).

Encyclopedia of the New Economy. http://hotwired.lycos.com/special/ene/ (accessed on May 5, 2002).

Globalization.com http://www.globalization.com/index.cfm (accessed on May 5, 2002).

Nobel e-Museum. http://www.nobel.se/index.html (accessed on May 5, 2002).

United States Department of Labor Home Page. http://www.dol.gov/ (accessed on March 5, 2002).

chapter three *Education*

1990: **March 5** Channel One, a commercial-ly sponsored television news program designed for use in high school class-rooms, makes its formal debut in four hundred schools across the country.

1990: **December 7** Astronauts onboard the space shuttle *Columbia* beam a class-room lesson on star formation and celestial radiation from space to forty-one middle school students gathered at NASA centers in Alabama and Maryland.

1991: The Centers for Disease Control (CDC) releases a report based on a 1990 survey that found that almost one in five American high school students sometimes carried a gun, knife, or other weapon to school.

1991: **November 1** A University of Iowa physics graduate student, distraught over his failure to win an academic award, shoots and kills five people and critically injures another.

1992: **January 18** A seventeen-year-old high school student shoots and kills an English teacher and a janitor and holds classmates hostage in Grayson, Kentucky.

1992: **June 24** With a 5-4 majority vote, the U.S. Supreme Court rules that prayers delivered at a public high school graduation violated First Amendment principles separating church and state.

1993: Tensions rise at the University of Pennsylvania when five black sorority sisters charge a white student with racial harassment after he called them "water buffalo."

1993: **September 8** The Boston Teachers' Union votes in favor of a new contract that would directly tie teachers' pay to improvements in student performance.

1993: **November 3** The school board in Minneapolis, Minnesota, votes unani-mously to hire a consulting firm to run the city's schools.

1994: **April 12** A ten-year-old shoots and kills an eleven-year-old classmate on their elementary school playground in Butte, Montana.

1994: **June 5** Michael Kearney, a ten-year-old boy, becomes the youngest Amer-ican to graduate from college when he receives a bachelor's degree with a major in anthropology from the Uni-versity of South Alabama in Mobile.

1995: **March 3** The Cleveland, Ohio, public school system is put under state control by a federal judge because of its $125 million debt.

1995: **August 12** Shannon Faulkner becomes the first woman to attend The Citadel in Charleston, South Carolina, as a member of its Corps of Cadets. She drops out of the school six days later.

1996: **August 15** Three professors are killed at San Diego State University when a graduate student opens fire with a handgun at the defense of his engineering thesis. His thesis had been rejected once before.

1996: **November 15** The public school system in Boston, Massachusetts, announces it will stop using racial preferences in its admissions process after a lawsuit brought by the father of a white girl who was denied admission to the elite Boston Latin School. The prospective student's entrance exam scores were higher than 103 black and Hispanic students who were granted admission to the school.

1997: **February 8** President Bill Clinton announces the Department of Educa-tion will issue grants to public schools to help them connect to the Internet.

1997: **December 1** A fourteen-year-old boy opens fire on his classmates at Heath High School in West Paducah, Kentucky, killing three girls and injuring five others.

1998: **March 24** Two youths, ages thirteen and eleven, embark on a fatal shooting spree at their junior high school in Jonesboro, Arkansas. Five people—four students and a teacher—are killed in the gunfire, and ten others are wounded.

1998: **October 22** President Clinton signs a bill expanding federal aid to charter schools while also setting stricter standards the schools must meet to qualify for federal funding.

1999: **April 20** At Columbine High School in Littleton, Colorado, two boys shoot and kill twelve fellow students and a teacher, and seriously wound more than twenty other classmates before committing suicide.

1999: **August 11** The Kansas State Board of Education decides that the state will no longer test students on evolutionary theory, though it may still be taught.

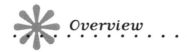

Overview

One of the major concerns of parents during the 1990s was their children's protection while at school. When asked about schools' shortcomings, parents named the safety and welfare of their children as their greatest fear. The media repeatedly covered incidents of shootings by students not only in high schools but also in middle schools across the country. Senseless deaths of students and teachers horrified the nation. While test scores and improved achievement remained key educational goals, increasingly schools were forced to wrestle with violent students. Metal detectors, police presence, and routine locker searches became common in schools across the country. Urban, suburban, and rural schools alike all faced similar student safety issues.

As funds were being spent to tighten security in schools, they were also being spent to improve learning. The bleak picture of public education—violence, low scores on standardized tests, run-down school buildings—convinced many parents to explore other education options for their children. These alternatives included homeschooling, charter schools, and school vouchers.

Of the more than forty million American school-aged children in the late 1990s, thirty million were enrolled in public schools. Some experts estimated, however, that more than one-half of those parents would have enrolled their children in private schools if they could have afforded the high cost of tuition. Even parochial schools that charged relatively low yearly tuition rates of several thousand dollars were too pricey for middle- and working-class American families. These families supported the idea of receiving monetary vouchers to defray part of the tuition cost, not only at private schools but also at successful public schools outside their district. As the voucher concept became more popular, its opponents made their views widely known in courts, the media, and political forums. School choice as an issue was hotly debated throughout the decade.

Another education topic debated across the country for several decades was the issue of teaching evolutionary theory in public schools as an explanation of human origins. Many parents and religious groups objected to the emphasis placed on the theory accepted by the vast majority of scientists around the world. They believed that creationism, the theory based on the Biblical account of creation, should be given equal treatment in public classrooms. The debate regarding teaching the two theories was still unresolved when the decade ended.

At the level of higher education, affirmative action suffered a major blow in the 1990s. The policy, which had been created to increase opportunities for women and minorities in the workplace and in university admissions, came under fire in several states. Voters decided to repeal laws supporting the policies, drastically changing the racial makeup of student bodies at public universities. In turn, many courts across the nation upheld these controversial decisions by voters.

Walter H. Annenberg (1908–) Walter H. Annenberg, philanthropist and publisher, placed his extraordinary wealth firmly behind American public schools in 1993 when he announced the Annenberg Challenge Grant. The program provided five hundred million dollars in matching grants to public elementary and secondary schools across the country to improve the effectiveness of public education. It helped initiate reform in some of the nation's largest and most troubled school districts, as well as rural schools. By 1998, more than two thousand schools with nearly 1.5 million students had been involved in the Annenberg Challenge. *Photo reproduced by permission of the Corbis Corporation.*

Marian Wright Edelman (1939–) Marian Wright Edelman, founder and president of the Children's Defense Fund, has devoted her entire life to improving the welfare of children. Through her organization, she has tried to focus national attention on issues such as child health care, teen pregnancy, and others. In June 1996, Edelman played a major role in the formation and presentation of the first annual *Stand for Children* rally held in Washington, D.C. More than three thousand people attended the event. *Photo reproduced by permission of the Corbis Corporation.*

Bill Nye (1955–) Bill Nye started hosting a zany half-hour television program, *Bill Nye the Science Guy,* on Public Broadcasting System (PBS) channels across the nation in 1993. Although aimed at fourth graders, it appealed to people of all ages. In a format filled with "cool" music, stunts, and flashy graphics, the program took one important scientific concept each episode and used it as the learning objective for that show. Interviews with "way cool" scientists and bizarre demonstrations of how science is applied in everyday life became hallmarks of Nye's critically acclaimed show. *Photo reproduced by permission of AP/Wide World Photos.*

Richard W. Riley (1933–) Richard W. Riley became secretary of education under President Bill Clinton in 1993. He immediately set about developing a national education system driven by high academic standards. He focused on improving public schools, showing little support for vouchers or other incentives for parents to move their children to private schools. Riley asserted that the improvement of public education was dependent on the elevation of teaching to the status of a first-class profession. Among his many proposals was a three-step system for the preparation of teachers similar to that required of doctors: internship, residency, and certification. *Photo reproduced by permission of Archive Photos, Inc.*

❖ SHOOTINGS AND VIOLENCE IN SCHOOLS

Perhaps more than any other educational issue in the 1990s, the subject of violence in schools made news. A rash of gun violence in seemingly safe suburban schools around the country indicated that violence was not just an urban problem. Although the high-profile cases involved suburban, white, middle-class students, the majority of children killed at school lived in lower income areas and were African American.

For the first time since the early 1970s, violence was seen as one of the major problems in schools. According to the annual Gallup poll taken on attitudes toward the public schools, violence topped the list of Americans' concerns in 1998. In a mad search for the solution, few educators and politicians could agree on the root of the problem, blaming movies, television, rap music, video games, parents, schools, and lack of religion.

For years, isolated incidents of shootings, stabbings, and other school violence saddened the country. Most Americans believed these random acts of violence occurred mainly in poor schools, sometimes the product of a single deranged individual Not until several similar mass shootings occurred around the country during the late 1990s did the country focus on the problem as a national concern. Americans all asked the same questions: How could such events happen? Was no one aware of the intentions of these shooters? How could they get their hands on these weapons of destruction? What was their motivation?

Many leading politicians pointed accusatory fingers at the film and music industries. They believed violent scenes in films and offensive lyrics in rap and rock music prompted young people to mimic such behavior. In response, executives in both industries claimed that violent messages in films or songs were not the problem, since millions of people saw such films and listened to such recordings without committing acts of violence. The problem, they believed, lay with the federal government, which had failed to pass gun-control laws and similar legislation.

In 1998, in the wake of numerous school shootings, President Bill Clinton (1946–) stated in one of his weekly radio addresses that youths' exposure to violence in movies, on television, and in video games warped their perceptions. He called on the U.S. Congress to pass a proposed juvenile crime bill that would ban young people convicted of violent offenses from purchasing guns for the rest of their lives. Gun-control advocates called for stricter restrictions on the sale and use of firearms. Opponents

U.S. High School Dropout Percentage: 1995

Total, all races	12.0
Total, white	8.6
Total, black	12.1
Total, Hispanic	30.0
Male, all races	12.2
Male, white	9.0
Male, black	11.1
Male, Hispanic	30.0
Female, all races	11.7
Female, white	8.2
Female, black	12.9
Female, Hispanic	30.0

of such measures argued that new laws should focus on people who committed crimes with guns, not on the guns themselves.

As the debate between the two sides continued, the deadliest school shooting in American history took place. On April 20, 1999, gunfire erupted in a suburban high school in Littleton, Colorado, near Denver. Seniors Eric Harris, eighteen, and Dylan Klebold, seventeen, killed thirteen people and sent more than twenty others to hospitals with gunshot and shrapnel wounds before turning their weapons on themselves. Nationwide television broadcast images of students fleeing from the building with their hands above their heads. Not shown were wounded victims still inside the school.

Hundreds of police officers throughout the Denver area surrounded the school. Some students called their parents, the police, and television stations on cellular phones from inside the building. Nearby schools were locked and students were prohibited from entering or leaving the campus for hours. Law enforcement officers found dozens of explosives, including a twenty pound propane bomb, in the school and parking lot. For several days, Federal Bureau of Investigation (FBI) agents and police SWAT teams searched for and removed explosive devices that Harris and Klebold had hidden throughout the building.

❖ ALTERNATIVE EDUCATION AND SCHOOL CHOICE

As reports of violence and mediocre achievement scores plagued American schools in the 1990s, parents increasingly looked for other schooling options for their children. School-reform advocates, tired of fighting within the system, sought to develop alternatives to the public school system. Still others argued that the best way to hold the public schools accountable for performance was through consumer choice, giving parents the option of sending their children to the private school of their choice at taxpayer expense. Public debate on the options continued throughout the decade. Although fewer than one-half of the people in an annual Gallup Poll favored allowing students to choose a private school at public expense, the numbers who agreed with the idea grew during the 1990s, from 26 percent in 1991 to 44 percent in 1998.

In the last two decades of the twentieth century, homeschooling became popular. Nearly 80 percent of those parents who chose to homeschool their children did so because they distrusted the public school system. Others did so because they wanted to be more involved in the education of their children. Homeschooled children numbered over one million by the late 1990s.

Fifteen crosses were placed on a hill above Columbine High School in Littleton, Colorado, in memory of those who died in the school's 1999 shooting. Black plastic drapes the crosses of the gunmen, Dylan Klebold and Eric Harris.
Reproduced by permission of AP/Wide World Photos.

Strengths of homeschooling include the prolonged time spent as a family, a higher degree of meaningful interaction between parents and children, an ability to illustrate that education does not end when the bell rings or when vacation arrives, and a more individualized program of study.

Critics of homeschooling argued that children do not develop the normal social skills arising from interaction with fellow students. Parents of homeschooled children countered that a typical classroom does not resemble a normal social setting. They pointed out that many of the interactions in a classroom—bullying, elitism, teasing, conformism due to peer pressure—are not healthy.

Another alternative to public schools that arose in the 1990s was charter schools. These public institutions operate under a contract negotiated between the school's organizers (teachers or parents, for example) and a sponsor (such as a local school board, a state board of education, or a university) that oversees the provisions of the charter. The charter describes the school's instructional plan, specific educational outcomes, and its management and financial plan. Charter schools receive state funding, but are independent legal entities that have the ability to con-

A Wisconsin family conducts a home school session in their basement. Nearly 80 percent of those parents who choose to homeschool their children do so because they distrust the public school system. Reproduced by permission of AP/Wide World Photos.

In December 1996, the local school board in Oakland, California, unanimously decided that the district would recognize black English as a separate language as opposed to a dialect of English or a form of slang. As a distinct language, Ebonics (from the words ebony and phonics) could be used to teach students in their primary language with the aim of improving achievement for the city's African American children. Proponents of the plan asserted that Ebonics contained linguistic elements from African languages and that many African Americans had retained speaking patterns from their African roots. By allowing teachers to recognize the separate language, supporters argued, more effective teaching could take place.

Critics immediately condemned the move, saying it undercut the need to teach standard English to African American children. They accused the district of trying to access funds aimed at non-English-speaking students. Civil rights leader Jesse Jackson urged the district to reverse its decision, arguing that black students who could not speak standard English would have difficulty finding jobs. A week after the school board announced its decision, U.S. Secretary of Education Richard Riley confirmed that the Clinton administration would not accept the designation of Ebonics as a separate language.

The following month, the Oakland school board altered its plan in the wake of rising criticism that they had insulted the learning abilities of African American children. Although the issue of Ebonics disappeared from the national scene, the underlying problems the school board sought to address continued.

trol their own finances. Most charters are granted for a specified amount of time. If the schools fail to meet the conditions of their charters, they are closed.

Minnesota enacted the first charter school law in 1991. By the end of 1998, over one thousand charter schools were operating in twenty-seven states plus the District of Columbia; only thirty-two charter schools had failed. The demand for charter schools remained high: 70 percent of these schools reported a waiting list. Each year, more states passed charter school legislation, and several of them altered their laws to increase the numbers of charters that could be granted.

Goals 2000: Educate America Act of 1994

1) All children will start school ready to learn.
2) The nation's high school graduation rate will increase to 90 percent.
3) Students in grades 4, 8, and 12 will demonstrate competency in nine core academic areas.
4) The United States will be first in international comparisons of math and science achievement.
5) Adult literacy will be universal.
6) Schools will be free of drugs and violence.
7) Teachers will have access to continual professional-development opportunities.
8) All schools will increase parental involvement in their children's education.

A 1996 amendment to the act had the following provisions:

1) School districts in states that were not participating in Goals 2000 were allowed to apply for aid on their own if they had the approval of the state education agency.

There were no typical charter schools. They operated differently depending on the state legislation under which the charter school was approved. The specific schools targeted diverse student populations and instituted vastly different educational philosophies. On average, charter schools enrolled far fewer students than public schools, although the student demographics were similar. Since they were small, charter schools often provided more individualized attention for their students.

Critics of charter schools argued that the schools drew attention and resources away from necessary reform efforts in public schools. They also pointed out that charter schools were one step away from public approval of vouchers for school choice.

One of the initial ideas for school choice promoted issuing monetary vouchers (documents typically valued between $2,500 and $5,000) to parents of school-age children, usually in troubled inner-city school districts. Parents could then apply the vouchers toward the cost of tuition at private schools, including parochial or religious schools. Although suc-

2) A requirement that states submit school-improvement plans to the U.S. Secretary of Education was removed. States were still to draft plans based on challenging standards and aligned assessments, but could get money by promising that it would be spent properly.

3) Provisions specifying the membership of state and local panels charged with drafting the state and local plans were deleted.

4) The National Education Standards and Improvement Council was formally eliminated.

5) References to "opportunity to learn" standards for measuring school services, including a requirement that states create opportunity-to-learn "standards or strategies," were removed.

6) No district, state, or school "shall be required...to provide outcomes-based education or school-based health clinics."

7) The Goals 2000 law will not "require or permit any state or federal official to inspect a home, judge how parents raise their children, or remove children from their parents."

cessfully implemented in several states, vouchers continued to cause controversy throughout the nation.

Critics of vouchers argued against the use of public funds to support religious schools. These opponents also asserted that public schools could not improve if funds constantly were diverted away from the schools. In their strongest argument, the critics pointed out that vouchers would not necessarily equalize educational opportunities in America: Rich families would use the vouchers to help pay part of the tuition at the best schools; poor families could only use the vouchers, worth only a few thousand dollars, to help cover the costs at less desirable private schools.

During the decade, court battles abounded to abolish various controversial voucher systems across the nation. In June 1998, the Wisconsin Supreme Court upheld that state's voucher program, which included religious schools. In April 1999, the Maine Supreme Court ruled that state-funded school vouchers could not be used to send children to religious schools. The battle over vouchers continued beyond the end of the 1990s.

The Walls Came Tumbling Down: Women in Military Schools

· ·

S hannon Faulkner wanted to attend the prestigious South Carolina military college, The Citadel. In 1993, she applied and was accepted to the all-male, 152-year-old institution—but she was female. Faulkner had deleted all gender references in her college application. When school officials discovered they had admitted a female applicant, they quickly withdrew their offer of enrollment.

Accepted on her qualifications, but denied entrance because of her gender, Faulkner sued the college, believing it was unconstitutional to discriminate against women by denying them a Citadel education. As one of

two all-male, publicly funded military academies in the country, The Citadel braced for a long court battle. Armed with attorneys and the support of the National Organization for Women (NOW), Faulkner brought national attention to the issue.

Faulkner's efforts to enroll in the traditional academy were hotly debated by people across America. The nation's other all-male, state-funded military academy, Virginia Military Institute (VMI), also faced a court battle

❖ **TEACHING DARWIN: THE EVOLVING CONTROVERSY IN PUBLIC SCHOOLS**

One educational battle that had arisen in previous decades continued unchecked well into the 1990s: the debate between the teaching of evolutionary theory and creationism in public schools. The modern theory of evolution, as proposed by English naturalist Charles Darwin (1809–1882), holds that present-day life on Earth evolved from previously existing life-forms through a process of gradual, continuous change over millions of years. Almost all scientists consider evolution one of the most fundamental and important general concepts in the biological sciences. Creationism is a theory about the origin of the universe and all life in it based on the account of creation given in the Old Testament of the Bible. Creationism holds that Earth is less than ten thousand years old, that its physical fea-

with the U.S. Justice Department. During the two-and-a-half-year legal proceedings, Faulkner, her family, and her lawyers faced many threats from
angry opponents.

In January 1994, Faulkner became the first woman to attend day classes at
The Citadel. However, she was not allowed to join the corps of cadets or
participate in any military training. After a long legal battle, Faulkner finally
won the right to become the first female cadet at The Citadel. On August
12, 1995, she began her career at the military academy. Less than a week
later, having been unprepared for the physical rigors all cadets face upon
entering, Faulkner dropped out.

In June 1996, the U.S. Supreme Court ruled that VMI must admit women
or give up its state funding because its single-sex admission policy violated the equal protection clause of the U.S. Constitution's Fourteenth
Amendment. The Citadel, in response, also yielded and changed its
admission policy. Of the four female cadets who enrolled in The Citadel
in the fall of 1996, two quit mid-year amid allegations of sexual harassment and safety issues (ten male cadets faced disciplinary action in connection with those incidents). In the spring of 1999, Nancy Mace became
the first female graduate of The Citadel. *Photo reproduced by permission of AP/Wide
World Photos.*

tures such as mountains and oceans were created as a result of sudden
calamities, and that all life on the planet was miraculously formed as it
exists today by a divine creator. Because creationism is not based on any
presently held scientific principles, members of the scientific community
dismiss it as a possible theory of how the universe was created.

In 1981, lawmakers in Louisiana had passed legislation requiring that
both evolutionary theory and creationism be taught equally in public
schools. In 1987, and repeatedly thereafter, the U.S. Supreme Court ruled
that such a requirement was invalid because creationism was a statement
of theology, not biology. This setback did not stop determined members of
school boards across the country from trying to sidestep the ruling. They
continued to try to delete evolution from the curriculum or to make sure
that it was countered by presenting creationism as an alternative.

Technology in the Classroom

The growth of technology during the 1990s affected schools around the country. Computer technology, once a luxury, became a necessary addition to every school in the nation. As the decade progressed, so did expectations of students, parents, and employers about each school's ability to teach students the necessary skills to function in an increasingly technical world.

Teachers comfortable with computer technology praised the Internet. Online discussions with students in foreign countries, publishing opportunities for students, and access to government information led teachers to encourage students to explore cyberspace. Consequently, the Internet became a favored educational tool across the country. Between 1994 and 1998, Internet access in public schools increased from 35 percent to 89 percent, and the percentage of classrooms with access went up from 3 percent to 51 percent.

Recognizing that schools with severely limited resources would lag even further behind, President Bill Clinton took steps to help these schools provide Internet access to their students. In 1996, as part of the Telecommunications Act, the Universal Service program was born. Commonly known as the "E-rate," the program structured a series of discounts from telecom providers for schools and libraries to help defray the cost of telecommunications and Internet technologies. The details of the program were left to the Federal Communications Commission (FCC), which inaugurated the program in May 1997.

The program received over 62,000 applications in its first two years of operation, making it clear that schools and libraries saw a great need for increasingly their accessibility to the Internet. Originally slated to have a budget of $2.25 billion per year, the FCC cut the program's funding for the first year to only $1.2 billion, thereby significantly reducing the number and amount of grants available to schools.

In August 1999, the Kansas State Board of Education adopted new standards for the teaching of science, which effectively removed any discussion of evolution as an explanation for human origins. The decision was widely praised by religious conservatives. Scholars, science educators, and those who believed in the constitutional separation of church and state were appalled.

Although the decision surprised and outraged many scientists, politicians, journalists, and parents, national polls suggested that 68 percent of Americans wanted creationism taught in conjunction with evolution as equally viable theories about the origins and development of life on Earth. As many as 40 percent of respondents favored teaching creationism instead of evolution. Of those polled, only 7 percent thought that no Supreme Being played a role in either the creation or evolution of life on the planet.

Not long before the school board in Kansas took action, similar quarrels had erupted in California, Colorado, Idaho, Illinois, Iowa, Nebraska, Oregon, and Washington. The state textbook committees in Alabama and Oklahoma had already inserted disclaimers into science books stating that evolution was an unproven theory that students were by no means obliged to accept as fact. The attorney general of Oklahoma subsequently ordered the disclaimer removed. The Kansas State Board of Education decision thus only intensified an ongoing dispute.

❖ **AFFIRMATIVE ACTION TAKES A BEATING**

Affirmative action, in which preferential treatment is given to women and minorities to compensate for previous discrimination in employment and college admissions, suffered a major setback in the 1990s. In November 1996, California voters passed Proposition 209, making the state the first in the nation to ban state-sponsored affirmative action programs. When opponents of the proposition took their case all the way to the U.S. Supreme Court, the Court refused to hear the case.

Also in 1996, the U.S. Fifth Circuit Court of Appeals in New Orleans, Louisiana struck down an affirmative action admissions policy at the University of Texas School of Law in Austin. That decision effectively banned preferential admissions based on race at state-run schools in Texas, Louisiana, and Mississippi—the three states under the jurisdiction of the appeals court.

Those in favor of affirmative action pointed to enrollment figures at schools affected by Proposition 209 as justification for the need of affirmative action programs. The law school at the University of California, Los Angeles reported that only twenty-one African American students had been admitted for the 1997–1998 school year—the lowest total in nearly thirty years and down 80 percent from the previous year. The law school at the university's Berkeley campus had admitted only fourteen African American students for the coming school year, down from seventy-five the previous year. Both law schools said that similar drops in admissions had occurred among Hispanic applicants.

The debate over affirmative action was not limited to California but raged on across the country. While voters in California debated Proposition 209, twenty-six states drafted similar initiatives. In 1998, 58 percent of the voters in Washington state approved Initiative 200, banning state and local agencies from granting preferential treatment on the basis of race, ethnicity, or gender when admitting students to state schools, hiring for state jobs, or awarding state contracts.

 For More Information

BOOKS

Edelman, Marion Wright. *The Measure of Our Success: A Letter to My Children and Yours.* New York: HarperPerennial, 1993.

Manegold, Catherine S. *In Glory's Shadow: Shannon Faulkner, the Citadel, and a Changing America.* New York: Knopf, 2000.

Nye, Bill. *Bill Nye the Science Guy's Big Blast of Science.* Cambridge, MA: Perseus Publishing, 1993.

Nye, Bill. *Bill Nye the Science Guy's Consider the Following: A Way Cool Set of Science Questions, Answers, and Ideas to Ponder.* New York: Hyperion Press, 2000.

Zimmer, Carl. *Evolution: The Triumph of an Idea.* New York: HarperCollins, 2001.

WEB SITES

Children's Defense Fund. http://www.childrensdefense.org/ (accessed on May 9, 2002).

Goals 2000 Legislation and Related Items. http://www.ed.gov/G2K/ (accessed on May 9, 2002).

Institute for Creation Research. http://www.icr.org/ (accessed on May 9, 2002).

National Center for Education Statistics Home Page. http://nces.ed.gov/ (accessed on May 9, 2002).

National Center for Science Education. http://www.natcenscied.org/ (accessed on May 9, 2002).

U.S. Department of Education. http://www.ed.gov/index.jsp (accessed on May 9, 2002).

chapter four *Government, Politics, and Law*

1990: **January 3** Manuel Antonio Noriega Moreno, dictator of Panama (1983–89), is arrested on drug smuggling, racketeering, and money laundering charges.

1990: **August 2** Saddam Hussein's Iraqi army invades Kuwait. President George Bush freezes Iraqi and Kuwaiti assets in U.S. financial institutions; the United Nations calls on Iraq to withdraw.

1990: **August 7** The United States sends the 82nd Airborne Division and several fighter squadrons to the Middle East.

1991: **January 16** U.S. warplanes and missiles attack Iraq and occupied areas of Kuwait in Operation Desert Storm, launching the Persian Gulf War.

1991: **March 3** Rodney King is beaten by Los Angeles police officers following a high-speed automobile chase.

1991: **October 11** The Clarence Thomas nomination hearings begin before the U.S. Senate Judiciary Committee. Anita Hill, a former colleague of Thomas's, accuses the Supreme Court nominee of sexual harassment.

1992: **February 1** President Bush and Russian President Boris Yeltsin proclaim a formal end to the cold war.

1992: **April 29** Rioting erupts in south central Los Angeles after the four police officers accused of beating Rodney King are either acquitted or given light sentences. The rioting lasts until May 2.

1992: **December 24** As his term in office nears its end, President Bush pardons all former Reagan officials who were involved in the Iran-Contra scandal in the mid-1980s.

1993: **February 26** The World Trade Center in New York City is bombed, killing six people and injuring more than one thousand. Several Islamic extremists are later arrested and convicted for carrying out the attack.

1993: **April 19** Federal agents storm the Branch Davidian compound near Waco, Texas, ending a fifty-one-day siege in a fiery inferno and killing eighty men, women, and children.

1993: **July 20** White House deputy counsel Vincent W. Foster Jr. is found dead of an apparently self-inflicted gunshot wound in Fort Marcy Park, Virginia.

1994: **February 3** President Bill Clinton ends the trade embargo against the Republic of Vietnam, which had been put into effect in 1975.

1994: **May 6** Paula Corbin Jones files suit in federal court charging President Clinton with having committed sexual harassment against her while he was governor of Arkansas.

1994: **December 5** Newton "Newt" Gingrich (R-Georgia) is chosen to be Speaker of the House.

1995: **April 19** A bomb explodes at the Alfred P. Murrah Federal Building in Oklahoma City, Oklahoma, killing 168 people and injuring more than 500.

1995: **Summer** Monica Lewinsky serves as an intern at the White House.

1995: **October 3** O. J. Simpson is acquitted of the murders of his former wife Nicole Brown Simpson and her friend Ronald Goldman.

1996: **January 26** First Lady Hillary Rodham Clinton testifies before a grand jury in connection with the Whitewater real estate investment investigation

1996: **April 3** Theodore "Ted" Kaczynski is arrested by FBI agents at his Montana cabin in connection with the Unabomber case.

1996: **December 5** President Clinton appoints Madeleine Albright as the first female secretary of state.

1997: **January 17** Newt Gingrich is found guilty of ethics violations ten days after being reelected as speaker of the House of Representatives.

1997: **May 27** The U.S. Supreme Court rules unanimously that President Clinton could not delay the civil suit brought against him by Paula Corbin Jones.

1997: **June 2** Timothy McVeigh is convicted of charges in connection with the Murrah Federal Building bombing in Oklahoma City.

1998: **January 21** President Clinton denies an alleged affair with former White House intern Monica Lewinsky.

1998: **September 11** Independent counsel Kenneth W. Starr submits his report to Congress on possible offenses by President Clinton that could lead to impeachment.

1998: **December 19** The U.S. House of Representatives passes two Articles of Impeachment against President Clinton.

1999: **January 7** The U.S. Senate impeachment trial of President Clinton begins, with Chief Justice William Rehnquist presiding.

1999: **February 12** President Clinton is acquitted by the Senate on both Articles of Impeachment.

1999: **April 12** A U.S. district court judge holds President Clinton in contempt of court for giving misleading information when he was asked about his relationship with Monica Lewinsky. It is the first time in U.S. history a sitting president in held in contempt of civil court.

War, scandal, political reform, terrorism, and civil rights marked the 1990s. The cold war (the period of heightened tension after World War II between the former Soviet Union and the United States) ended with the collapse of communism early in the decade. In response, President George H. W. Bush called for a "new world order" in which global security would be based on diplomacy and international commerce. After the cold war, however, the world was dangerous and unpredictable. U.S. military and political institutions had to scramble to deal with new and unexpected threats to American and global security.

In August 1990, Iraqi president Saddam Hussein challenged U.S. interests in the Persian Gulf region when his troops invaded Iraq's oil-rich neighbor, Kuwait. Believing that allowing such behavior to go unchecked only invited further aggression, Bush mobilized U.S. forces and demanded that Iraq withdraw from Kuwait. Bush also won approval for military actions from the United Nations Security Council and built a worldwide coalition of support, garnering cooperation and assistance from allies and former adversaries. In January 1991, when the U.S.-led alliance invaded the region in Operation Desert Storm, Iraqi resistance collapsed before the overwhelming military might. Kuwait was freed, but Hussein remained in power throughout the rest of the decade.

The end of the Persian Gulf War did not end hostilities around the world. Long-simmering ethnic and religious tensions in the Balkans, the African continent, and other areas around the world exploded into violence and genocide (systematic killing of an entire national or ethnic group). The Balkan peninsula, especially the former Yugoslavia, became an ethnic powder keg as national and religious identity provided the basis for violent confrontations. U.S. soldiers joined multinational peacekeeping forces to restore and maintain peace around the world.

America was not immune to the spreading violence. Several major terrorist attacks on American soil occurred during the decade, including the 1995 bombing of a federal building in Oklahoma City, Oklahoma. There were also attacks at the World Trade Center in New York City (1993), the Olympics in Atlanta (1996), and Central Intelligence Agency (CIA) headquarters in Langley, Virginia (1993). These assaults shocked the public and caused law enforcement and government agencies nationwide to increase and update security measures. Federal and state governments began to search for new ways to track and prosecute the activities of hate groups. In one such case, a fringe religious group in Waco, Texas, engaged federal law enforcement officers in a fifty-one-day standoff that resulted in almost eighty deaths. The incident sparked public debate and a federal investigation into the handling of the case by government officials.

The public's concern over ethics in government focused on President Bill Clinton even before his 1992 presidential election. Clinton's alleged involvement in the Whitewater land development scheme, his public denials and subsequent admission of an affair with a young White House intern, and the highly political nature of his 1998 impeachment by the House of Representatives and 1999 trial before the Senate led Americans to question the personal and political ethics of both the executive branch and Congress.

Other trials during the decade further divided Americans, especially along racial lines. The trial of four white Los Angeles police officers in the beating of African American motorist Rodney King ended in a not-guilty verdict that sparked a vicious riot in south central Los Angeles. In what many labeled the "trial of the century," former football star O. J. Simpson was found not guilty in the murders of his former wife and her male friend. While many African Americans celebrated the verdict, many white Americans sat stunned, believing Simpson committed the murders.

Madeleine Albright (1937–) Madeleine Albright was appointed U.S. secretary of state in 1997, becoming the first woman to hold the post and the highest-ranking woman ever in the executive branch. For four years previously, she served as the U.S. representative to the United Nations. Her diplomatic and political skills were well regarded around the world. Albright had a reputation as a plain-spoken and aggressive defender of U.S. interests. Yet she was also well known for her ability to talk to many different people with varying political agendas and to get them to agree on difficult issues. *Photo reproduced by permission of the Corbis Corporation.*

George H. W. Bush (1924–) George H. W. Bush served as the forty-first president of the United States from 1989 to 1993. In office, he quickly established the reputation of specializing in foreign affairs while having little real interest in domestic issues. The dramatic end of communism, the invasion of Panama, and the Persian Gulf War marked his presidency. In perhaps his finest hour, Bush organized a worldwide, UN-sanctioned coalition against Iraq for its invasion of Kuwait. At the end of the Gulf War, he enjoyed a virtually unprecedented public approval rating of 91 percent. *Photo courtesy of the Library of Congress.*

Hillary Rodham Clinton (1947–) Hillary Rodham Clinton, the forty-second first lady of the United States, used her position as few previous first ladies had done. In 1993, she chaired a task force charged with producing a health care reform plan. Although the plan was not adopted by the U.S. Congress, Clinton continued her leadership role, traveling the globe to bring attention to women's issues, children's issues, and health care. In 1995, Clinton served as honorary chair of the American delegation to the United Nations' Fourth World Conference on Women held in Beijing, China. *Photo reproduced by permission of the Corbis Corporation.*

Johnnie Cochran (1937–) Johnnie Cochran gained national notoriety in 1994 when he became a member of O. J. Simpson's legal defense team. Along with fellow defense attorney F. Lee Bailey, he developed the "race card" strategy as a chief defense tactic. He called attention to recorded racist remarks made by a police detective involved in the murder investigation. Cochran also provoked one of the prosecuting attorneys into having Simpson try on a pair of blood-stained gloves, which clearly did not fit, eventually leading the jury to find Simpson not guilty. *Photo reproduced by permission of AP/Wide World Photos.*

Newt Gingrich (1943–) Newt Gingrich, who served as a U.S. representative from Georgia beginning in 1979, was elected Speaker of the U.S. House of Representatives late in 1994. In this powerful position, he led fellow Republican representatives' efforts to implement the so-called Contract with America. Gingrich influenced the political agenda between 1994 and 1996, helping Republicans gain control of the House. In 1997, he was fined three hundred thousand dollars for violating House ethics rules regarding the use of tax-exempt foundations for political purposes. In November 1998, he resigned his seat in the House. *Photo reproduced by permission of AP/Wide World Photos.*

H. Ross Perot (1930–) H. Ross Perot, an extremely successful businessman from Texas, ran for the presidency of the United States in 1992 and 1996 as the candidate from his newly formed Reform Party. Though he lost both elections, he made a credible showing, and his Reform Party continued to influence American politics. Many Americans agreed with Perot's view that a self-serving elite dominated government, ignoring the problems of average citizens. At the end of the decade, Perot's political vision continued to draw support across the country. *Photo reproduced by permission of Archive Photos, Inc.*

Colin Powell (1937–) Colin Powell had become the youngest man and the first African American to hold the country's top military office, chairman of the Joint Chiefs of Staff. He was an instrumental figure in Operations Desert Storm and Desert Shield, and he served as President Bush's key adviser during the Persian Gulf War in 1991. He was credited with skillfully balancing the political objectives of President Bush and the strategy needs of General Norman Schwarzkopf. In 1994, he served as part of a three-person team that helped avert a military invasion of Haiti by U.S. troops. *Photo reproduced by permission of AP/Wide World Photos.*

Janet Reno (1938–) Janet Reno became the first female U.S. Attorney General when she was sworn in to the post in 1993. Noted for her strong-willed, straightforward manner, she had a reputation for being willing to take difficult stands. Some of her decisions angered members of Congress, who repeatedly called for her to step down from her post. She offered to resign after the Waco incident, but President Clinton refused to accept her resignation. Despite being embattled on all sides, Reno served longer in her position than any attorney general in the previous thirty years. *Photo reproduced by permission of the Corbis Corporation.*

◆ *Topics in the News* . . . .

❖ PERSIAN GULF WAR

On August 2, 1990, the Iraqi army moved into neighboring Kuwait and seized control of the oil-rich nation, claiming they were rightfully reclaiming their own territory. The unprovoked and unexpected action surprised the United States and Western Europe. Kuwait supplied oil to Europe and Asia; Iraqi control of Kuwaiti oil fields, along with Iraq's own immense oil resources, would put much of the world at the mercy of its highly unpredictable leader, Saddam Hussein. The invasion threatened not only the world supply of oil but also political stability in the Middle East.

Western allies immediately sought a United Nations (UN) resolution condemning the action of Iraq. Hussein was surprised by this reaction because scarcely a week before, U.S. ambassador to Iraq April C. Glaspie had told him that the border dispute between Iraq and Kuwait was an Arab issue. Hussein thought he had been clear about his intentions; the ambassador thought Hussein was merely restating an old territorial dispute. Once Iraq acted, however, the West did not ignore the situation.

President George H. W. Bush (1924–) contended that Iraq's action threatened U.S. political and economic positions in the Persian Gulf region. First, Iraqi militarism threatened the balance of power in the Middle East. For decades, the United States had tried to find a peaceful balance in the hostile relations between the region's Arab states and Israel. The Iraqi invasion could upset that balance, uniting Arab states in opposition to the West and Israel. Bush recognized the need for a swift response and dubbed his plan Operation Desert Shield.

On August 19, 1990, the UN declared the Iraqi takeover of Kuwait invalid, and on August 25 it authorized military action. Bush also worked quickly to support Saudi Arabia, which was threatened by Hussein's action and which Bush needed as a staging area for military actions against Iraq. Ultimately Bush was able to get not only Saudi Arabian cooperation, but also help from most Arab states in the region. Bahrain, Egypt, Kuwait, Oman, Qatar, Saudi Arabia, and Syria all contributed soldiers and munitions in the fight against Iraq. Jordan, which felt particularly vulnerable because of its geographic location between Israel and Iraq, chose to remain neutral.

The United States told Iraq that if it did not withdraw its armies from Kuwait by January 15, 1991, the United States and UN-backed alliance of nations would retaliate. At this point the coalition moved five hundred thousand land, air, and naval forces into the Middle East and prepared to fight.

Iraq was well prepared for war. Many observers considered the military might of Iraq to be the strongest in the Arab world. Hussein's elite Republican Guard had a fearsome reputation as a first-rate fighting force. The Central Intelligence Agency (CIA) also had evidence that Iraqi agents were developing biological, chemical, and nuclear weapons. It was assumed that Hussein would not hesitate to use them.

After the U.S. Congress passed a resolution supporting armed intervention in Kuwait, the next phase of the effort—Operation Desert Storm—began. On January 17, 1991, U.S. missiles and warplanes launched attacks on Iraq's capital city, Baghdad, and other military targets. The army had projected that the war would last many months and cost thousands of lives. Luckily, the estimates were greatly overstated. The missile attacks were very effective; by the time ground troops invaded Iraq and Kuwait on February 24, 1991, they met little resistance. On February 28, President Bush ordered a cease-fire, and on March 3, Iraq formally accepted a peace agreement.

The peace agreement imposed a no-fly zone over northern Iraq (forbidding Iraqi aircraft from flying over the area), installed economic sanctions, and required inspections of military installations by UN teams. It also allowed Hussein to remain in charge in Iraq. Unbowed, Hussein continued to test the resolve of the United States and UN by failing to cooperate with UN inspection teams as they looked for evidence of nuclear, bio-

A medic helping a solider to an airlift during in the Persian War in 1991.
Reproduced by permission of the Corbis Corporation.

logical, or chemical weapons of mass destruction and generally resisting all efforts to undermine his power. In his eight years in office, Bush's successor President Bill Clinton (1946–) was no more successful against Hussein's resistance than Bush had been. The decade ended as it had begun, with Hussein still in power in Iraq.

❖ PEACEKEEPING MISSIONS: AMERICA AS THE WORLD'S POLICE FORCE

The belief that a United Nations (UN) peacekeeping coalition was the best way to control world unrest was strengthened immediately following the 1991 Persian Gulf War. However, that belief was constantly tested throughout the remainder of the decade. With the collapse of the Communist Soviet Union, the United States became the world's only remaining superpower. The role of world's police force—leading and coordinating international intervention in conflicts around the world—increasingly fell to the United States. Sometimes these so-called peacekeeping missions led by the United States under UN sponsorship succeeded. Often, they did not.

For decades, war and strife had plagued the African country of Somalia, which lies along the northeast coast of the continent. In 1991, a rebel group in the north announced its secession from Somalia and proclaimed itself the Somaliland Republic. The ensuing civil war combined with the worst African drought of the century created devastating famine. Public health officials estimated in the fall of 1992 that up to one-third of Somalia's population was in danger of starvation; the dead already numbered tens of thousands.

In December 1992, the United Nations passed a resolution to deploy a U.S.-led international military operation to Somalia to safeguard a massive fifteen-month relief effort. By the end of December, faction leaders had pledged to stop fighting. Operation Restore Hope, as the relief effort was labeled, quickly spread throughout the country, and violence decreased dramatically. By early 1993, more than thirty-four thousand troops from twenty-four UN member countries (75 percent of them from the United States) were deployed in Somalia. Starvation was virtually ended, and some order had been restored. Yet little was done to achieve a political solution or to disarm the rebels.

Although the UN effort solved the problem of distributing relief supplies, Somalia still had no central government and few public institutions. Local warlords and their forces became increasingly bold. Danger to U.S. troops and other relief workers remained high. In October 1993, eighteen U.S. Army Rangers were killed and seventy-five were wounded in a firefight with rebel factions. President Bill Clinton (1946–), under pressure from the American public and other politicians, withdrew U.S. troops. After the withdrawal of the foreign peacekeeping troops, faction leader General Muhammad Farrah Aideed became the country's self-declared president. However, his rivals refused to bow to his authority, and unrest in the country continued.

Haiti is the world's oldest black republic and the second oldest republic in the Western Hemisphere (after the United States). It occupies the western half of the island of Hispaniola, the second largest in the Caribbean Sea. In 1990, Jean-Bertrand Aristide was elected president of Haiti. Upset by Aristide's popularity and his foreign policy, the military, under General Raoul Cédras, ousted him in October 1991. The United Nations then forged an agreement to return Aristide to the presidency in October 1993, but the military stalled and Cédras remained in power. Aristide appealed to the United States, and the Clinton administration responded with economic sanctions (penalties imposed as a result of breaking a law or violating an international policy) against the Haitian regime in May and June 1994.

In September 1994, as a last resort, the Clinton administration secured international support for a military invasion of Haiti to force Cédras from power. A U.S. invasion force was assembled and war seemed imminent. However, Clinton sent a special delegation composed of former president Jimmy Carter, Senator Sam Nunn of Georgia, and retired U.S. Army general Colin Powell to negotiate a peaceful solution to the crisis. As U.S. fighter planes were about to take off for Haiti, the Carter-led team reached an agreement with Cédras and war was averted. American forces peacefully took control of the country and, in October 1994, restored Aristide to power.

The resolution of the conflict in the former Yugoslavia was not so peaceful. The collapse of communist regimes in Eastern Europe in 1989 had a deep impact in Yugoslavia. By 1991, Yugoslavia was dissolved, and its former provinces of Slovenia, Croatia, Bosnia-Herzegovina, and Macedonia declared their individual independence. This left only Serbia and Montenegro together as a new Federal Republic of Yugoslavia.

The coalition government of Bosnia-Herzegovina had a very difficult time maintaining a spirit of ethnic cooperation with its neighbors. The Serbian and Croatian governments each wanted a temporary confederation with Bosnia as a transition to unification with their respective "mother states." The Bosnian Muslim party favored an independent united Bosnia and Herzegovina. Ultimately war broke out in Bosnia in mid-1992. While Serbs took over some 70 percent of the province, Croats kept control of western Herzegovina. The Croat's Muslim allies tried to resist Serbian attacks on predominantly Muslim cities and towns full of Bosnian refugees. The war destroyed over 60 percent of the homes in Sarajevo, the Bosnian capital, along with many historic buildings. Bombing and fires also damaged the environment.

Peacekeeping efforts in the region were made by the European Community, the United States, the United Nations, and the North Atlantic Treaty Organization (NATO). In July 1995, Bosnian Serbs overran areas under UN protection. In retaliation, NATO forces began air raids on Bosnian Serb positions in August 1995. The Bosnian Serb forces then started lifting their siege of Sarajevo, and agreed to negotiate over Bosnia's future.

Pressured by the air strikes and intense diplomacy, Serb officials joined leaders from Bosnia and Croatia on October 31, 1995, in Dayton, Ohio, for a round of peace talks. On November 21, 1995, the presidents of Bosnia, Croatia, and Serbia finally agreed to terms that would end the fighting in Bosnia after four years and an estimated 250,000 casualties. The agreement called for sixty thousand UN peacekeepers to prevent future conflicts. Despite the Dayton peace accords, the fighting in Yugoslavia continued into 1999, forcing peacekeeping forces to continue to patrol the embattled region.

❖ CONTRACT WITH AMERICA

The 1994 congressional elections resulted in a Republican landslide as many voters across the country, angered by President Bill Clinton's agenda, turned en masse to more conservative candidates. (Conservatives, often represented by the Republican Party, favor preserving traditional values and customs. They oppose any sudden change in the balance of power, and they believe the federal government should have limited control over the lives of average Americans. On the other hand, liberals, usually represented by the Democratic Party, favor a stronger central government. They support political reforms that extend democracy, distribute wealth more evenly, and bring about social progress.)

Much of the credit for the Republican success in that election can be attributed to Newton Leroy "Newt" Gingrich, the Republican representative from Georgia who rose through the ranks after his election to the U.S. Congress in 1978 to become Speaker of the House in 1994. That year, he seized the opportunity for leadership by promoting a conservative legislative agenda: the "Contract with America."

The Contract with America promised to pass eight legislative reforms in the first one hundred days of the 104th Congress and ten new laws in the following one hundred days. The Republicans promised to clean up

For decades, tobacco companies rarely lost health-related lawsuits. This trend changed in the 1990s as the tobacco industry paid out hundreds of billions of dollars in settlements, losing lawsuits filed by individuals, groups (class-action suits), cities, and states. As a result, cigarette prices soared. Smoking was made even more expensive as sales taxes on cigarettes were increased in an effort to discourage smoking and to raise revenue. State and federal agencies launched antismoking campaigns, primarily targeted at youth. Although adult smoking consistently declined during the decade, tobacco use increased among individuals under the age of eighteen. Smoking and tobacco use caused more than 430,000 deaths each year, and generated associated annual health costs of $100 billion.

On November 14, 1998, four of the largest American cigarette manufacturers and attorneys general in forty-six states reached an historic settlement. In the largest civil suit award in U.S. history, Philip Morris, R. J. Reynolds, Lorillard, and Brown & Williamson agreed to pay $206 billion to cover the medical costs of smoking-related illnesses. The states were scheduled to receive twelve billion dollars up front over the first five years. The rest would be paid in annual installments until 2025. In addition, the cigarette makers agreed to spend $1.7 billion on research aimed at discouraging smoking, especially among teenagers. The settlement also required that tobacco companies halt advertising on billboards and in transit stations, such as bus terminals and subways. Further, the companies were banned from selling clothing and merchandise that carried cigarette brand logos. This meant that cartoon characters such as Joe Camel could not be used in advertising. While the settlement was aimed at reducing smoking, it did not include any specific penalties if smoking did not decline. There were also no penalties if underage smoking increased.

Congress by reducing the number of committees, opening committee meetings to the public, requiring a three-fifths vote on tax bills, limiting the terms of committee chairs, and cleaning up budgeting processes.

While these congressional reforms were rather sweeping, the proposed legislative agenda was even broader. It included bills supporting a federal balanced-budget amendment, an anticrime package, programs to

Americans with Disabilities Act

Disabled Americans celebrated when President George Bush signed the Americans with Disabilities Act (ADA) in 1990. Affecting people from all walks of life, the bill prohibited discrimination against and provided support for the transportation, access, and telecommunication needs of the country's physically or mentally impaired population. Hailed as a major civil rights victory, the ADA provided guidelines on how schools, private businesses, and public institutions could accommodate the disabled. Although the new law was hailed as a positive step, schools and businesses everywhere had to begin planning adjustments to facilities, and services adversely affected their budgets.

discourage teen pregnancy, stronger child-support enforcement, income tax reform, and congressional term limits.

Each of these areas struck a chord with the American people. There was general agreement that the federal government had become too big, although there was little agreement on which areas should be cut. The Contract had the advantage of putting many pet projects of the Republican leadership into a framework that was easy to understand. Even congressmen who did not support a balanced-budget amendment or congressional term limits found it difficult not to sign the Contract. Democrats in the House were forced into the uncomfortable position of seeming to favor crime or teenage pregnancy if they opposed the Contract with America.

In the 1994 elections, the Republicans picked up several governorships and won an additional fifty-four seats in the House of Representatives and four seats in the U.S. Senate, gaining control of both chambers. Gingrich wasted no time in pushing his colleagues to implement the Contract with America. During the first one hundred days of the 104th Congress, nine out of ten proposed articles were adopted into law. Only the issue of term limits did not pass. Even President Bill Clinton (1946–) admitted defeat. He spent the next two years drafting moderate economic policies, which led to a booming economy, and softening his earlier liberal positions on such items as health care and homosexuals in the military.

1992: Year of the Woman

Women stormed onto the U.S. political stage in 1992. That fall, female candidates across the nation ran for Congress in record numbers. Five Democratic women were elected to the Senate: Barbara Boxer and Dianne Feinstein from California, Blanche Lambert Lincoln from Arkansas, Carol Moseley-Braun from Illinois, and Patty Murray from Washington. This influx increased the total number of women in the Senate to eight, while the House female membership rose to forty-eight representatives. Women across America also used their power in the voting booth to help elect Democratic presidential candidate Bill Clinton. The press quickly labeled 1992 as the "Year of the Woman."

Nonetheless, the media still tended to focus on trivial stories about first ladies Barbara Bush and Hillary Rodham Clinton rather than on serious issues related to women candidates. Election coverage often focused on male candidates. When so many women swept into Congress and Clinton was elected, many feminists thought that significant women's issues would at last be addressed. These hopes were short-lived, however; in 1994 the Republicans won a majority of seats in both the House and Senate. Their conservative members announced their "Contract with America," including significant new restrictions on abortion rights and welfare benefits.

❖ TRIALS OF A PRESIDENT: SCANDALS AND IMPEACHMENT

The administration of President Bill Clinton (1946–) was plagued by scandals and allegations of corruption. Clinton's alleged abuses of women, money, and power led to his 1998 impeachment hearings in the U.S. House of Representatives and a subsequent 1999 trial in the U.S. Senate. Although he became only the second president in U.S. history ever impeached by the House of Representatives, he was not convicted in his trial before the Senate.

From the beginning of his 1992 campaign, rumors swirled about Clinton's extramarital affairs. The first scandal concerned a woman named Gennifer Flowers, who alleged that she had a twelve-year affair with Clinton while he was the governor of Arkansas. She also claimed that he got her a job in the state government because of their relationship. Clinton refused to admit to the affair and went on national television with his wife,

Presidential Election Results: 1992

Presidential/ Vice Presidential Candidate	Political Party	Popular Vote	Electoral Vote
William Clinton/ Albert Gore	Democrat	44,909,806 (43.01%)	370 (68.8%)
George Bush/ J. Danforth Quayle	Republican	39,104,550 (37.45%)	168 (31.2%)
H. Ross Perot/ James Stockdale	Independent	19,742,240 (18.91%)	0 (0.0%)
Andre Marrau/ Nancy Lord	Libertarian	291,631 (0.28%)	0 (0.0%)
Other		378,531 (0.36%)	0 (0.0%)

Hillary Rodham Clinton, claiming that even though they had had problems in their marriage, they loved and supported each other. The appearance defused the rumors and seemed to end Clinton's personal problems, at least until after his inauguration.

The second scandal broke shortly after President Clinton's first inauguration in 1993. His political opponents convinced a young woman in Arkansas, Paula Corbin Jones, to go public with an allegation of sexual harassment that allegedly had occurred in 1991. Jones claimed that at a political function held at a hotel, Clinton had invited her up to his room and then sexually propositioned her. Clinton denied the allegation. Rather than disappearing, however, Jones filed suit in federal court on May 6, 1994, initially seeking seven hundred thousand dollars in damages for malicious conduct. Clinton's attorneys wanted the suit dismissed on the grounds that a sitting president could not be tried in a civil case. Both sides contested the case all the way to the U.S. Supreme Court, which ruled in May 1997 that the trial could proceed. Finally, in November 1998, an out-of-court settlement was reached in which Clinton agreed to pay Jones $850,000 while not admitting to any wrongdoing.

Other alleged scandals, involving money and power, also stained the reputation of the Clinton administration. Chief among these was Whitewater, an Arkansas land development project in which Bill and Hillary

Presidential Election Results: 1996

Presidential/ Vice Presidential Candidate	Political Party	Popular Vote	Electoral Vote
William Clinton/ Albert Gore	Democrat	47,402,357 (49.24%)	379 (70.4%)
Robert Dole/ Jack Kemp	Republican	39,198,755 (40.71%)	159 (29.6%)
H. Ross Perot/ Pat Choate	Reform	8,085,402 (8.40%)	0 (0.0%)
Ralph Nader/ Winona LaDuke	Green	685,128 (0.71%)	0 (0.0%)
Harry Browne/ Jo Jorgensen	Libertarian	485,798 (0.50%)	0 (0.0%)
Other		420,194 (0.44%)	0 (0.0%)

Rodham Clinton had invested money during the late 1970s. Ten years later, the project fell through, and the federal government spent $60 million to rescue investors in a failed savings-and-loan institution that had ties to the project. Throughout the next decade, federal investigators tried to determine whether and to what extent the Clintons were involved in the failure of the savings and loan.

President and Mrs. Clinton eventually were found to be innocent of any charges in the Whitewater case—the investigation of which cost American taxpayers million of dollars. But the independent prosecutor, Kenneth W. Starr, began to examine unrelated charges that Clinton had committed perjury when he testified in federal court during the Jones hearing, possibly lying under oath about an extramarital affair he was alleged to have had with a White House intern named Monica Lewinsky. A grand jury (a panel of jurors called to decide whether sufficient grounds exist for criminal prosecution) was convened to hear testimony about these allegations.

On August 17, 1998, Clinton appeared before the grand jury (via closed-circuit television monitor) to answer questions about his relationship with Lewinsky. It was the first time in American history that a sitting president had to testify before a grand jury. That evening, Clinton gave a televised speech to the American people in which he said he had had an

Bill Clinton

Bill Clinton dominated the U.S. political landscape for most of the 1990s. He was the first president born after the end of World War II (1939–45) and the first elected after the end of the cold war. Clinton began his two-term presidency intending to tackle several high-profile political issues including national health insurance, the budget, civil rights, and education. His presidency was forever tainted, however, by his personal behavior. Clinton evaded questions about his draft status during the Vietnam War (1954–75), whether he had smoked marijuana as a young man, his numerous extramarital affairs, and his lies and half-truths about his sexual behavior that led to his impeachment. His presidency succeeded in many ways, yet Americans believed he could have accomplished even more.

William Jefferson Blythe IV was born in Hope, Arkansas, on August 19, 1946. Three months before his birth, his father Bill Blythe, was killed in an

automobile accident. When he was four years old, his mother married Roger Clinton; her son took the Clinton name when he was in high school. Clinton was an accomplished student and saxophonist, talented enough to earn music as well as academic scholarships. He attended Georgetown University in Washington, D.C., graduating with a degree in international affairs in 1968. After graduation, Clinton was awarded a prestigious Rhodes Scholarship to study at Oxford University in England.

"improper relationship" with Lewinsky. This statement contradicted what Clinton had told the public emphatically some seven months before: that he " ...did not have sexual relations with that woman [Lewinsky]."

After some debate, on October 4 the House Judiciary Committee voted along strict party lines to recommend a full inquiry against the president into the allegations of perjury (lying under oath) and obstruction of justice (using his influence to cover up the alleged perjury). Four days later, the Republican-controlled House followed the committee's recommendation

After two years abroad, Clinton returned to the United States and began his legal studies at Yale University. While there, he met Hillary Rodham, also a promising law student (the couple married in 1975). After graduating from law school in 1973, he briefly taught law, as did Rodham, at the University of Arkansas. His first run for public office was an unsuccessful try at the Arkansas Third District congressional seat in 1974. Two years later, Clinton was elected state attorney general of Arkansas, and in 1978 he was elected governor when he was only thirty-two years old. He was defeated in his 1980 reelection bid, but came back and won the governorship again in 1982. He held it from that point until his 1992 run for the presidency.

In many ways, Clinton's two terms in office were successful. He presided over rapid and sustained economic growth, balanced the federal budget (after three decades of deficits), reformed welfare, and reduced crime. He also negotiated peace accords in the Middle East and Northern Ireland, implemented free-trade agreements including NAFTA, and created a national service program (AmeriCorps). Unfortunately, Clinton will be remembered as the president who was impeached by the House because of improper conduct with a young White House intern, and who was forced to admit publicly to embarrassing indiscretions, lies, and partial truths. Throughout the entire impeachment process, though, public opinion polls repeatedly indicated that while the American public had serious reservations about Clinton's character, they emphatically did not want him removed from office. *Photo reproduced by permission of the White House.*

and voted to begin hearings investigating possible grounds for impeachment (formally accused of serious misconduct). On December 19, the House, again voting along party lines, approved two articles of impeachment against the president: that he had lied before the grand jury and that he had obstructed justice.

Once a president is impeached by the House, the U.S. Senate then conducts a trial, with the senators serving as jurors, to determine whether the president should be convicted of "high crimes and misdemeanors" and removed from office. A two-thirds vote (sixty-seven senators) is required to convict. On January 7, 1999, the impeachment trial began in the Senate. On February 12, after closed hearings, the Senate found Clinton not guilty on both articles of impeachment. Article I, alleging perjury, was defeated on a forty-five to fifty-five vote. Article II, charging obstruction of justice, failed on a fifty-fifty tie. Polls taken during the trial had shown that most Americans neither supported impeachment nor a Senate trial of the president.

❖ TERRORISM: THE GROWING HATE MOVEMENT

The 1990s saw an increase of extremist demonstrations and violence across America, from marches by the white supremacist group Ku Klux Klan to murders and bombings. Tens of thousands of Americans joined various antigovernment and hate groups. Early in the decade, domestic terrorism rose to a level not seen since the activities of student radicals during the late 1960s and early 1970s. There were about five hundred active militia groups across the country, some with only a few members and others with thousands. Many of these militias were antigovernment, racist, and anti-Semitic (prejudiced against Jews). While most groups did not use violent tactics, some provided tragic examples of how far extremist individuals and organizations were willing to go in waging war against the government and other targets of their hate—racial and ethnic minorities.

One of the longest-running violent-crime cases within the Federal Bureau of Investigation (FBI), active for seventeen years, involved a series of fatal bombings. It was called the Unabomb case, a code name selected because one of the bombs exploded aboard an airline with a similar name (although most of the bombs were set off on university campuses). Beginning in 1978, the serial bomber, later identified as Theodore "Ted" Kaczynski, mailed or concealed sixteen homemade explosive devices, killing three people and injuring twenty-three others.

A crucial development in the Unabomber case occurred in early 1996 when the bomber sent a manuscript to the *New York Times* and the *Washington Post*. With FBI approval, both papers published the thirty-five-thousand-word treatise. The Unabomber argued that the purpose of the bombings was to call attention to, among other things, the ill effects of technology on modern society and traditional values. Publication of the manifesto led David Kaczynski to link it with earlier writings of his estranged brother Ted, who was living as a recluse near a small town in Montana.

On April 3, 1996, Ted Kaczynski, a former mathematics professor at the University of California, Berkeley, was arrested by FBI agents at his cabin. On June 18 he was formally charged with ten counts relating to the transportation and mailing of explosive devices that killed or injured victims in California, New Jersey, and Connecticut. In January 1988, he confessed to the bombings and was subsequently sentenced to life in prison without the possibility of parole.

As millions of television viewers watched on April 19, 1993, a massive inferno erupted in Texas between federal agents and a well-armed religious fringe group known as the Branch Davidians. After a fifty-one-day siege, the exchange of gunfire and subsequent blaze killed eighty people, including four federal agents.

Events leading up to this fiery conclusion began on February 28. Ninety heavily armed Bureau of Alcohol, Tobacco, and Firearms (ATF) agents unsuccessfully attempted to serve a warrant on the leader of the Branch Davidians, David Koresh, at their residential compound outside of Waco, Texas. The search-and-arrest warrant, resulting from nearly a year of investigation and surveillance, alleged that the Davidians possessed illegal firearms and were converting semiautomatic rifles into machine guns. (Later investigations found that the group had indeed stockpiled almost four hundred firearms, including forty-eight machine guns.) During the seven-week standoff, the activities at Waco dominated national news, and Davidian leader Koresh became a household name.

After months of negotiations, the standoff finally ended when agents drove federal tanks and armored vehicles through the walls of the compound and fired dozens of gas canisters into the building, attempting to force out the Davidians. Following the assault, smoke poured out of the structure and within minutes the entire compound was engulfed in flames. Seventy-six group members died, including twenty-five children under the age of fifteen. At least two dozen victims, including Koresh, were later discovered to have died from gunshot wounds, either self-inflicted or caused by someone else in the compound. Nine Davidians escaped by fleeing the building.

On April 19, 1995, exactly two years after the final assault on the Waco compound, a homemade bomb, made with ammonium-nitrate fertilizer and hidden in a rented truck, exploded at the Alfred P. Murrah Federal Building in Oklahoma City, Oklahoma. The explosion killed 168 people and injured more than 500 others—the most deadly domestic terrorist attack in U.S. history. The Murrah Building housed a variety of federal agencies, as well as a day care center for the children of federal employees. Nineteen children under the age of five were killed in the blast. Because of the timing, federal prosecutors speculated that the bombing likely stemmed from strong antigovernment feelings that had been inflamed by the Branch Davidian debacle.

An hour and a half after the blast, Timothy James McVeigh was arrested on an unrelated weapons violation during a routine traffic stop. On April 21, McVeigh, a U.S. Army veteran of the Persian Gulf War and a Bronze Star recipient, was charged by federal authorities in connection

with the bombing. Terry Lynn Nichols, also a former soldier, was charged as an accomplice on May 10. On August 11, both McVeigh and Nichols were charged by a grand jury with murder, conspiracy to commit murder, conspiracy to use a weapon of mass destruction, and use of a weapon of mass destruction. The murder charges pertained to the eight federal agents who were killed in the Oklahoma City explosion. In October, U.S. Attorney General Reno authorized federal prosecutors to seek the death penalty in both cases.

The judge overseeing the trial ordered the two men to be tried separately. McVeigh's lawyer argued that the evidence against McVeigh was weak and that another man, known only as "John Doe 2," actually carried out the bombing. The jury did not believe the defense and convicted McVeigh on all charges on June 2, 1997. McVeigh later was sentenced to death by lethal injection. He was executed on June 11, 2001.

Although investigators never placed him at the bomb scene, Nichols also was convicted on December 23, 1997, as McVeigh's accomplice. He was subsequently sentenced to life in prison without the possibility of parole.

Not all terrorist attacks on United States soil were perpetrated by American citizens. On February 26, 1993, an explosion rocked the World Trade Center in New York City, killing six people and injuring more than one thousand. When the bomb went off, more than fifty thousand people were inside the 110-story complex. The bomb, placed in a parking garage beneath the structure, contained approximately twelve hundred pounds of explosives. The attack caused $500 million in damage. At the time, it was the most heinous act of foreign terrorism on American soil.

Federal investigators arrested four men—foreign nationals from the Middle East belonging to various Muslim fundamentalist groups—within a few weeks of the attack. These religious extremists claimed to be pursuing a jihad, or holy war, against America—defining the term in a violent way that horrified most mainstream followers of Islam. In March 1994, each of the suspects was convicted and sentenced to 240 years in prison. Just over three years later, two other men were tried and convicted on charges of conspiracy and murder. They, too, received 240-year prison terms. The bombing investigation began to reveal the wide extent to which anti-American foreign terrorists lived and operated in the United States.

❖ RACE RELATIONS ON TRIAL: RODNEY KING AND O. J. SIMPSON

High-profile court cases dominated the headlines during the 1990s, but none captured the nation's attention more so than two racially tainted

*OPPOSITE PAGE
The Alfred P. Murrah Federal Building in Oklahoma City, Oklahoma, after a bombing in 1995.
Reproduced by permission of AP/Wide World Photos.*

cases in greater Los Angeles, California: the Rodney King beating trial and the O. J. Simpson murder trial. These cases also demonstrated that relations between black and white Americans were still strained, even three decades after the civil rights movement began.

On March 3, 1991, Rodney Glen King, who had served a year in prison for theft and aggravated assault, was driving on a California freeway with two friends. When Los Angeles Police Department (LAPD) officers attempted to stop him for speeding, King, who had been drinking and was still on parole, led the police on a high-speed chase and was finally forced off the road. During his arrest, several officers used excessive force against King. They claimed that the six-foot-three-inch King had charged them and resisted arrest; King contended that he was afraid of the armed white officers and had attempted to defend himself.

While the arrest was in progress, unknown to anyone at the scene, residents of a nearby apartment complex were awakened by the noise. One man videotaped part of the incident. Excerpts from the tape, showing a group of white police officers beating a black man lying on the ground, played repeatedly on television news programs around the world. King became an international symbol of police brutality and of the deep divide between white and black justice.

Less than two weeks after the incident, four LAPD officers were charged with unlawful assault and use of excessive force. The trial, which was moved out of Los Angeles at the request of defense attorneys to Simi Valley, a nearby suburban city with a predominantly white population, began in February 1992. After six weeks of testimony and six hours of deliberation, the jury found the officers not guilty. The end of the trial, however, only sparked more violence.

Between April 29, when the verdict was announced, and May 3, south central Los Angeles, a low-income area populated largely by minorities, was engulfed in chaos. Violence, looting, and mayhem ensued, as enraged roving black crowds attacked passersby—whites, Latinos, Asians, and other blacks, many of whom lived and worked in the area. Order was restored only after California's governor called in the National Guard. The toll from the civil unrest was devastating: more than fifty people dead, more than four thousand injured, more than one thousand businesses destroyed, and an estimated $1 billion in property damage.

In response to the King verdicts and the subsequent outrage of the south central Los Angeles community, the U.S. Justice Department filed federal charges against the four officers for violating King's civil rights. In April 1993, two of the four officers were found guilty of this charge and sentenced to serve thirty months in a federal correctional camp.

Three years after the King beating, Los Angeles and the nation once again faced racial divisions over a jury verdict. This time, however, the individual found not guilty was Orenthal James "O. J." Simpson, a retired African American football star, sports announcer, and popular television personality. Many Americans were shocked to learn of Simpson's arrest on June 12, 1994, as the prime suspect in the brutal murders of his former wife Nicole Brown Simpson and her friend Ronald Goldman outside her suburban L.A. home. The victims, both white, had been repeatedly stabbed, but there were no witnesses to the assault. Simpson claimed he was en route to Chicago when the crimes were committed.

Nonetheless, five days later police charged Simpson with the murders, citing a trail of evidence linking him to the scene of the crime. The evidence included a bloody glove found outside the murder scene that allegedly matched one found at his estate. Simpson did not surrender immediately. Instead, he and his lifelong friend Al Cowlings led police on a chase down a Los Angeles expressway while the nation watched the drama unfold on live television. The two men led police on a 60-mile,

A blurry video camera shot of police officers beating Rodney King in Los Angeles, California, in 1991. **Reproduced by permission of AP/Wide World Photos.**

O.J. Simpson, with his
lawyers, during his 1995
murder trial. *Reproduced by
permission of AP/Wide
World Photos.*

low-speed chase through southern Los Angeles that ended at Simpson's
Brentwood estate.

By the time the trial began on January 23, 1995, Simpson had hired a
team of celebrity lawyers—including Johnnie L. Cochran Jr., F. Lee Bailey,
Robert Shapiro, and appeals expert Alan M. Dershowitz. The media
referred to this group of attorneys as the "Dream Team." The prosecution
portrayed Simpson as jealous, controlling, and abusive (several years earlier he had pleaded no contest to abusing his wife). Evidence linking Simpson to the crime, however, was largely circumstantial: There was no murder weapon and no witnesses placed the defendant at the crime scene. The
prosecution did introduce several experts who testified that DNA (the
genetic material in an organism) samples from blood found at the crime
scene matched Simpson's DNA profile.

Simpson's lawyers argued that he did not have the opportunity to
commit the crimes and that the evidence presented was not only circumstantial but also may have been planted by racist LAPD officers. Lawyer
Johnnie Cochran then went even further, suggesting to the majority-black
jury that there was a widespread conspiracy against African Americans in
the justice system. He compared Simpson, a murder defendant, with Rodney King, a victim of police brutality.

In 1991, renowned U.S. Supreme Court Justice Thurgood Marshall (1908–1993) retired. To fill the vacant position, President George H. W. Bush nominated another African American—conservative federal appeals court judge Clarence Thomas. Democrats in the U.S. Senate (which has the power to accept or reject the nomination) viewed the nomination with dismay. Although they favored another justice who was a member of a racial minority, they also realized that Thomas was not the liberal jurist that Marshall had been. Republicans tended to support Thomas's nomination while Democrats did not. The bipartisan U.S. Senate Judiciary Committee was therefore divided when it sent Thomas's nomination to the Senate floor for a final vote.

Just as the full Senate was about to vote, the committee reopened its hearings because charges of sexual harassment had been leveled against Thomas by University of Oklahoma law professor Anita Hill. Testifying before the all-male committee and a nationwide television audience, Hill described in graphic detail Thomas's inappropriate statements and advances. She claimed that Thomas had sexually harassed her in the early 1980s while both had worked in the Office for Civil Rights—ironically, one of the chief federal law enforcement agencies for combating race and gender discrimination. For nine hours, Hill maintained her composure while answering questions from the senators about intimate and embarrassing details of the sexual harassment.

When given the opportunity to respond to Hill's allegations, Thomas denied all the charges. He then accused the Judiciary Committee of a

"high-tech lynching" and denounced committee Democrats as racists for reviewing the issue. He further claimed that Democrats had targeted him for political reasons because he was a black conservative.

On October 15, 1992, the full Senate voted fifty-two to forty-eight to confirm Thomas's nomination—the narrowest approval margin for any Supreme Court nominee in American history. *Photo reproduced by permission of AP/Wide World Photos.*

On October 2, 1994, three hours and forty minutes after receiving the case, the jury informed the presiding judge they had reached a verdict. Fearing a replay of the civil disturbances after the 1992 King verdict, the judge delayed the reading until the next day to give the police department time to prepare. On October 3, with millions of Americans watching on television or listening to the radio, the verdict was announced—Simpson was found not guilty. The verdict shocked many white Americans who had become convinced of Simpson's guilt. It elated many African Americans who were equally convinced he had been framed by a racially biased justice system.

The following year, the families of Nicole Brown Simpson and Ronald Goldman filed a civil suit against Simpson, charging that he was liable for their deaths. The burden of proof is lower in a civil case than in a criminal case, and the victims' families wanted Simpson held accountable for what they saw as his clear guilt. In February 1997, the jury in the case ruled against Simpson, awarding the families $8.5 million in damages.

 For More Information
· ·

BOOKS

Aaseng, Nathan. *The Impeachment of Bill Clinton.* San Diego, CA: Lucent Books, 2000.

Cothran, Helen, ed. *War-Torn Bosnia.* San Diego, CA: Greenhaven Press, 2001.

Kent, Zachary. *The Persian Gulf War: "The Mother of All Battles."* Berkeley Heights, NJ: Enslow Publishers, 1994.

Powell, Colin, with Joseph E. Persico. *My American Journey.* New York: Random House, 1995.

Toobin, Jeffrey. *The Run of His Life: The People v. O. J. Simpson.* New York: Random House, 1996.

WEB SITES

Clinton Presidential Center. http://www.clintonpresidentialcenter.com/ (accessed on May 12, 2002).

CNN-O. J. Simpson Trial. http://www.cnn.com/US/OJ/index.html (accessed on May 12, 2002).

Dave Leip's Atlas of U.S. Presidential Elections. http://www.uselectionatlas.org/USPRESIDENT/frametextj.html (accessed on May 12, 2002).

Frontline: The Gulf War. http://www.pbs.org/wgbh/pages/frontline/gulf/ (accessed on May 12, 2002).

Frontline: Waco-The Inside Story. http://www.pbs.org/wgbh/pages/frontline/waco/home.html (accessed on May 12, 2002).

George Bush Presidential Library and Museum. http://bushlibrary.tamu.edu/ (accessed on May 12, 2002).

ICPR-The Bombing of the World Trade Center in New York City. http://www.interpol.int/Public/Publications/ICPR/ICPR469_3.asp (accessed on May 12, 2002).

Time & CNN-The Unabomb Trial. http://www.time.com/time/reports/unabomber/index.html (accessed on May 12, 2002).

Time.com-The President on Trial. http://www.time.com/time/daily/scandal/ (accessed on May 12, 2002).

Time.com-Timothy McVeigh. http://www.time.com/time/2001/mcveigh/ (accessed on May 12, 2002).

chapter five *Lifestyles and Social Trends*

1990: Robert Bly's *Iron John* is published, giving a boost to the growing men's movement.

1990: January 1 Maryland becomes the first state to ban the sale of cheap handguns known as Saturday Night Specials.

1990: November 1 Under pressure from environmental groups, McDonald's agrees to replace polystyrene containers with paper wrappers.

1991: February 14 Homosexual and unmarried heterosexual couples begin registering under a new law in San Francisco to be recognized officially as "domestic partners."

1991: September 5 to 7 Naval and Marine aviators attending the thirty-fifth annual Tailhook convention assault dozens of women, including fourteen fellow officers at a hotel, in a drunken ritual called "the gauntlet."

1991: October In New York City, the first Planet Hollywood restaurant opens.

1992: June 9 William Pinckney becomes the first African American to sail solo around the world.

1992: August 11 The Mall of America, the biggest shopping complex built in the United States, opens in Bloomington, Minnesota.

1992: November Filmmaker Spike Lee's movie *Malcolm X* debuts in theaters, helping create a market for T-shirts and baseball caps bearing a simple "X" honoring the slain 1960s leader of the Nation of Islam.

1993: January 18 The Martin Luther King Jr. national holiday is observed for the first time in all fifty states.

1993: February 2 Smoking is officially prohibited at the White House.

1993: April 25 Gay-rights activists and supporters march on Washington demanding equal rights for gays and lesbians and freedom from discrimination.

1994: August Sportswear designer Tommy Hilfiger unveils his first complete line of tailored men's clothing, showing classic styles in suits, sport jackets, and coats.

1994: September 3 In Alaska, a local Native American tribal council exiles two teenage Tlingit boys, who beat and robbed a pizza delivery man, to an uninhabited island for eighteen months.

1994: October 11 The Colorado Supreme Court strikes down an anti-gay-rights measures as unconstitutional.

1995: April 19 A bomb explodes in front of the Alfred P. Murrah Federal Building in Oklahoma City, Oklahoma, killing 168 people.

1995: June 21 The Southern Baptist Convention formally apologizes for its history of racism.

1995: October 16 Nation of Islam leader Louis Farrakhan leads the Million Man March in Washington, D.C.

1996: July 12 The U.S. House of Representatives votes overwhelmingly to define marriage in federal laws as the legal union of a man and a woman only, regardless of what individual states recognize.

1996: September 19 Internationl Business Machines (IBM) announces it will extend health benefits to partners of homosexual and lesbian employees.

1997: In a *Time*/CNN poll, 22 percent of Americans believe that aliens from outer space have been in contact with humans; another 13 percent believe that aliens have abducted human beings in order to observe them or perform experiments on them.

1997: March 26 Thirty-nine members of the Heaven's Gate religious cult commit suicide in their residence near San Diego. They anticipated being taken to a higher level of conscious-

ness in a flying saucer supposedly trailing the Hale-Bopp comet.

1997: June A pair of century-old Levi's jeans found in a mine shaft sell for twenty-five thousand dollars.

1998: February 10 A college dropout who had e-mailed threats to Asian students is convicted of committing the first "hate crime in cyberspace."

1998: October 16 Antigay protestors demonstrate outside the funeral of twenty-one-year-old Matthew Wayne Shepard, a gay student at the University of Wyoming, who died October 12 after having been beaten on October 7.

1998: December Khakis are everywhere, replacing denim jeans as the first choice in casual dress for both men and women.

1999: February 9 The Reverend Jerry Falwell warns in his *National Liberty Journal* that Tinky-Winky, a character on the popular children's television program *Teletubbies,* promotes a homosexual lifestyle.

1999: February 11 In a landmark ruling, a federal jury in Brooklyn holds gun manufacturers liable for shootings carried out with illegally obtained handguns.

Overview

The 1990s was a decade of extremes and contradictions. Americans built bigger and more elaborate homes and drove more expensive automobiles, then worked longer hours to pay for them. Americans spent more, borrowed more, and went more deeply into debt. They drank more coffee, smoked more cigars, and turned gambling into a national pastime. Children struggled to deal with the pressures of the adult world to which they were increasingly exposed, and many were forced to adjust to new stepfamilies. Meanwhile, a disturbing number of adolescent and teenage boys went on deadly shooting rampages that left dozens dead or wounded and a troubled nation asking why. Even as Americans decried the rise in gun violence, guns nevertheless found their way into more households during the 1990s than ever before. Men endured a crisis of masculinity. Gays and lesbians came closer to entering the American mainstream, yet they often faced violent assaults and an antigay backlash.

Mass shootings, many of them involving children or teenagers, dominated American headlines during the decade. There was a growing sense among many Americans that no one was safe from unpredictable gun violence. Yet the attitudes of Americans toward guns remained ambivalent. The percentage of U.S. households owning guns increased while membership in the National Rifle Association (NRA) declined. Legislation such as the Brady Handgun Violence Prevention Act (1993) was offset by the passage of right-to-carry gun laws in more than thirty states.

The male crisis and the crusade for gay rights also made headlines. Pressured to be masculine in a culture that no longer valued traditional codes of manhood, many heterosexual men felt troubled and lost. Trying to create a movement to reclaim their masculinity, some men went into the woods to chant and to beat on drums, hoping to resurrect the "wild man" within. The movement soon died out. On the other hand, homosexuals led a movement that made their presence felt in all aspects of public life during the 1990s. They even inserted themselves into the mainstream of U.S. politics. Nevertheless, although the majority of Americans surveyed in 1998 believed that homosexual relations were acceptable, violence and a legal backlash against gay rights occurred throughout the decade.

In a time of extremes and uncertainties, Americans sought out spiritual direction, not only returning to mainstream churches but also exploring an array of spiritual alternatives. New Age spiritualism waned and prospered during the 1990s. Although the numbers of Americans willing to identify themselves as New Age spiritualists declined, the popularity of such gurus as Deepak Chopra suggested that spiritualism continued to assert an influence behind the scenes in American life. Indeed, spiritualism surfaced in some unlikely settings. The phenomenon of "corporate spiritualism" transformed the workplace in many companies, large and small. It motivated employees by emphasizing their individuality, their obligations to their employer, and their responsibility for their own happiness and fulfillment.

A high point for many in the decade—an event that was both political and spiritual—was the Million Man March. Organized by Louis Farrakhan, the leader of the Nation of Islam, the march drew almost one million African American men to the Mall in Washington, D.C., for a day filled with speeches and sermons extolling the virtues of family and community responsibility. The peaceful, uplifting event was the largest assembly of African Americans in U.S. history.

Americans relaxed many standards during the 1990s, including those regarding fashion. Offices across the country adopted casual dress codes. Although employers at first allowed dress-down Fridays or casual days during summers only, many companies adopted casual dress as a full-time policy by the end of the decade. In addition, young people, influenced by a new style of rock music known as grunge, started to wear loose-fitting jeans, old flannel shirts, and T-shirts. Some fashion designers incorporated these thrift store influences into their seasonal lines. Others catered to the growing hip-hop fashion movement that would come to dominate young America by the end of the decade.

Robert Bly (1926–) Robert Bly, one of America's most influential poets, published a book in 1990 that brought him to the attention of a far wider audience. *Iron John: A Book about Men* concerns the ancient rituals and traditional myths that humanity has used to connect with the masculine side of nature. The best-seller gave a great boost to the men's movement, which had sought to reconnect contemporary men with their own masculinity since the mid-1980s. *Photo reproduced by permission of Archive Photos, Inc.*

Deepak Chopra (1947–) Indian-born Deepak Chopra became one of the more influential New Age writers, educators, lecturers, and gurus to the rich and famous in America during the 1990s. Trained as a medical doctor, Chopra made believers out of thousands of Americans through a series of best-selling books, tapes, and lectures that delivered a message combining medical and spiritual advice. Critics accused him of being nothing more than a modern-day snake-oil salesman with an M.D. Nevertheless, his influence over many people was profound. By the end of the decade, Chopra had built a large and growing personal empire. *Photo reproduced by permission of AP/Wide World Photos.*

Ellen DeGeneres (1958–) Ellen DeGeneres, actor and comedienne, publicly revealed in April 1997 that she was a lesbian. At the same time, the character she played on her television show, *Ellen,* also came out of the closet, making the sitcom the first to include a gay lead character. When news of the impending episode was leaked in September 1996, it set off a national debate about gays both on television and in American life. Before the airing of the coming-out episode, antigay commentators threatened to boycott advertisers of the show. Despite this controversy, the show aired and garnered very high ratings. *Photo reproduced by permission of the Corbis Corporation.*

Louis Farrakhan (1933–) Louis Farrakhan, the best-known and most outspoken leader of the Nation of Islam (an African American organization whose members follow Islamic religious practice) had been dismissed by many as a hate-monger and an anti-Semite (person who discriminates against Jews). With his organization of the Million Man March in March 1995, however, Farrakhan seemed to move toward the mainstream of the civil rights movement. That one-day event, bringing together almost one million African American men and their sons, thrust Farrakhan into the spotlight as one of the most prominent black men in America. *Photo reproduced by permission of AP/Wide World Photos.*

Charlton Heston (1924–) Charlton Heston, Academy Award-winning actor, was elected president of the National Rifle Association (NRA) in 1998. As leader of this powerful organization that vigorously fights gun control legislation, Heston made remarks that some viewed as insulting toward women, minorities, and gays and lesbians. Undaunted, Heston and other members of the NRA continued to oppose any federal or state gun restrictions they believe denied their Second Amendment right to bear arms. *Photo reproduced by permission of Archive Photos, Inc.*

Tommy Hilfiger (1952–) Fashion designer Tommy Hilfiger made his mark in 1990s culture with his well-made, casual clothing sporting his distinctive red, white, and blue logo. He also placed "Tommy" across the front of T-shirts and an oversized "H" on sweaters. His popularity soared and his clothes appealed to a variety of people: youth and adults, blacks and whites, men and women. His ads promoted a sense of Americana, with women and men smiling and laughing in hometown settings. *Photo reproduced by permission of AP/Wide World Photos.*

Faith Popcorn (1947–) Professional futurist Faith Popcorn, born Faith Plotkin, spotted emerging trends and coined new terms to describe the 1990s. Major American corporations paid Popcorn and her firm, BrainReserve, millions of dollars to help them create marketing strategies, develop new products and revamp old products with new packaging. Her early predictions included "cocooning"—settling at home with take-out food and a video instead of going out to dinner and a movie. After her prediction became reality, the demand for take-out food boomed, creating an industry worth more than $28 billion by 1994. *Photo reproduced by permission of the Corbis Corporation.*

Marianne Williamson (1952–) Marianne Williamson emerged as a prominent spiritual counselor during the 1990s when she published her best-selling book *A Return to Love* in 1992. Throughout the decade, Williamson lectured to hundreds of thousands around America on topics ranging from love to relationships to philosophy to spirituality. She also published four other books that addressed such issues as politics and religion. At the end of the decade, she served as spiritual leader of the Renaissance Unity Church (formerly the Church of Today) in Warren, Michigan. *Photo reproduced by permission of AP/Wide World Photos.*

Topics in the News

❖ COFFEE, CIGARS, AND GAMBLING: FADS FOR THE '90S

In the 1990s, with the U.S. economy booming and the unemployment rate at its lowest level in more than two decades, Americans had money to spend. In what some economists called a "luxury fever," consumers spent their money on bigger and more expensive television sets, automobiles, and houses. Even the fads on which Americans spent money seemed luxurious.

Americans went crazy for coffee during the 1990s. They enjoyed gourmet blends at neighborhood coffeehouses and bought specialty coffees to drink at home. In the 1980s, such companies as Peet's Coffee & Tea and Starbucks Coffee helped to make gourmet coffees more widely available through mail order, thus enhancing their popularity. By the 1990s, coffee bars and coffeehouses appeared everywhere, including strip malls, airports, and bookstores. Coffee bars became convenient places for men and women to meet and socialize. The appeal of coffee during the decade came about in part because the beverage gave consumers an opportunity to treat themselves to an affordable luxury.

Among the most unexpected fads of the 1990s was the incredible popularity of premium cigars. Throughout much of the decade, annual sales and prices of premium cigars rose at unprecedented rates. Sales of premium cigars more than tripled between 1993 and 1998. Many industry experts traced the origins of the cigar boom to the introduction of *Cigar Aficionado,* a glossy magazine that promoted not only cigar smoking but also promised its readers an upscale lifestyle. Cigar smoking especially appealed to young men and women in their twenties and thirties. Consequently, smoke shops, cigar bars, and cigar-friendly restaurants and hotels did a brisk business. By the end of the decade, however, the demand for expensive, premium cigars had begun to decline. Prices fell dramatically, as did the value of stock shares. Companies that had begun to manufacture and sell cigars at the height of the boom declared bankruptcy, sold off their remaining inventory at a fraction of its former cost, and went out of business.

Many Americans with extra money to spend simply gambled it away. Gambling enjoyed phenomenal growth and spawned passionate protests during the decade. A survey conducted by the gaming industry found that 89 percent of Americans had no objection to casino gambling, even though 33 percent said they would not go to a casino themselves. Backers of gambling estimated that it brought in $1.4 billion in tax revenue to state and local government coffers. Critics, on the other hand, maintained that for every dollar contributed in taxes from the gambling venues, taxpayers spent at least three dollars on gambling-related expenses—from repairing streets around casinos to increasing police patrols to treating compulsive gamblers.

❖ THE MILLION MAN MARCH AND THE MEN'S MOVEMENT

On October 16, 1995, almost one million African American men, their sons, and their grandsons gathered on the Mall in front of the Washington Monument in Washington, D.C. Organized by Nation of Islam leader Louis Farrakhan, the Million Man March sent a message to the U.S. Congress that the black community stood strong against the conservative Republican majority in Washington, which promoted cuts in social programs for the poor and needy. In addition, participants in the event showed America that racism and inequality would neither be ignored nor tolerated. Most important, however, the march brought together black men of all ages from across the nation and across economic lines to hear a message of self-reliance, family and community responsibility, and respect for women.

The one-day event featured an extensive array of speakers: Farrakhan, National March director Benjamin Chavis, National Rainbow Coalition

Starbucks president Howard Behar posing in front of a newly opened shop in Beijing, China, in 1999. Reproduced by permission of Archive Photos, Inc.

president Jesse Jackson, Congressman (and future NAACP president) Kweisi Mfume, Congressional Black Caucus chairman Donald Payne, Detroit mayor Dennis Archer, entertainer Stevie Wonder, poet Maya Angelou, and civil rights figure Rosa Parks, among others. The marchers gathered on the Mall for more than seven hours, pledging themselves to continue the fight against racism in American and to take unity and responsibility back to their communities.

To many, Farrakhan seemed a surprising figure to be at the center of a gathering of black men focusing on unity and atonement. As leader of the Nation of Islam, he had long advocated a drug-free lifestyle, commitment to family, and economic self-empowerment for blacks. He was just as well known, however, for his harsh views about white people, Jews, and American culture. His commitment to Islam and black separatism put him at odds with the majority of leaders in the traditional civil rights movement. Indeed, some African American leaders decided to skip the event because of Farrakhan. Others embraced the ideals of the event without publicly supporting Farrakhan.

In the end, what mattered most to the participants of the march was the camaraderie and spirit of the huge and peaceful audience of black men. Though the media reported the march primarily as a political event, those in attendance later described the march as a spiritual event—a transforming moment of repentance, change, and renewal.

A more secular (nonreligious) movement for men also captured headlines during the decade. In 1990, poet Robert Bly published *Iron John: A Book About Men*. The best-seller addressed a growing uneasiness shared by many men of the baby-boomer generation (those born between 1946 and 1964). American society had changed, and this group of men felt they were missing something. Unlike their fathers and grandfathers, they had not fought in wars that clearly defined good and evil. They no longer worked in fields and factories filled with other men. As the twentieth century ended, the women's movement and the increasing complexity of family and social life demanded a redefinition of masculinity in America.

Bly's book provided a narrative based on ancient myths of the "wild man." Modern males, he suggested, had lost contact with their manhood. Young boys, raised by their mothers in the absence of father figures, were no longer learning about masculinity from other men. They thus grew up unable to understand themselves as men and unable to project the certainty of their forefathers. Modern men behaved irresponsibly, found themselves paralyzed by fear, and were generally frustrated in their pursuit of fulfillment. The answer, Bly suggested, was to be found in reestablishing

OPPOSITE PAGE
*The Million Man March held in Washington, D.C., in 1995. **Reproduced by permission of Archive Photos, Inc.***

bonds with other men. The "wild man" within, he asserted, had to be rediscovered and given an opportunity to grow strong.

Early in the decade, following Bly's advice, a few men sought to recover their masculine ideal by joining men's groups where they beat on

drums, chanted, and bonded with each other during weekend retreats in the woods. Unfortunately, this activity became more popular as an object of ridicule than as a serious social outlet. Lacking organization, the men's movement failed to establish itself within the fabric of American culture and soon died out.

❖ HOMOSEXUALITY AND THE NEW EXTENDED FAMILY

During the 1990s, unlike in previous decades, gays and lesbians tried to establish themselves in mainstream American life. At the same time, more Americans than ever before seemed to have accepted homosexuality. According to a 1998 *Time*/CNN poll, 64 percent of those questioned believed that homosexual relations were acceptable, while 36 percent thought them morally wrong. Twenty years earlier, 53 percent of Americans thought homosexual relations were morally unacceptable and only 41 percent found them permissible.

Many observers regarded the 1992 election of Democrat Bill Clinton as president as a turning point in the debate over gay rights, even though Clinton's support for gays sometimes wavered. Early in his first presidential term, Clinton had tried to lift the ban on gays serving in the U.S. military. When he finally compromised on the "Don't ask, don't tell" policy, which required all parties to stay silent regarding a soldier's sexual orientation, neither the military nor gays were satisfied. In addition, Clinton signed the Defense of Marriage Act in September 1996, which denied federal recognition of same-sex marriages. Yet Clinton also ended the federal policy of treating homosexuals as security risks, and was the first president to invite gay activists to the White House. The message Clinton sent was that gays not only were an integral part of America but that they also were becoming an important political constituency.

Even the Republican Party, which traditionally had refused acceptance to homosexuals, had to respond. In 1998, the chairman of the Republican National Committee (RNC), made a point of welcoming gays. A few conservative Republican senators, including presidential candidates Orrin Hatch and John McCain, quietly moved closer to gay support groups on issues such as hate-crime legislation but remained far apart on the issue of gay marriage.

Acceptance of gays and lesbians into mainstream society sparked vocal opposition and inspired vicious hate crimes. By the 1990s, violent assaults against homosexuals were nothing new—but the October 7, 1998, savage beating of university student Matthew Shepard in Laramie, Wyoming, shocked the nation. Shepard died from his injuries five days later. A *Time*/CNN survey conducted at the time of Shepard's murder

Joe Galluccio and Michael Galluccio exchange marriage vows in the Episcopal Church of the Atonement in Fair Lawn, New Jersey, in 1998. According to a Time/CNN poll, 64 percent of those questioned believed that homosexual relations were acceptable.
Reproduced by permission of AP/Wide World Photos.

revealed that 76 percent of those questioned favored increased penalties for those who commit hate crimes against homosexuals. By the end of the decade, forty-two states had passed hate-crime laws, and twenty-two specifically listed homosexuals as a specific class of potential victims.

Less violent, but no less injurious, was the growing backlash against gay rights in the decade. In 1998 in West Hartford, Connecticut, for example, the city council denied a gay couple's request to purchase a reduced-rate family pass to a municipal swimming pool. This incident, while hardly a major setback in the struggle for gay rights, nevertheless demonstrated to many observers a new set of barriers that gays faced. As the decade drew to a close, twenty-eight states had enacted legislation outlawing gay marriages. In February 1998, Maine became the first state to reverse a gay-rights ordinance prohibiting discrimination in housing and employment.

Although polls suggested that the majority of Americans accepted civil rights for gays, those same persons expressed uneasiness with the morality of homosexual behavior. In a 1998 *Newsweek* survey, 83 percent of respondents agreed that gays deserved equal rights to employment and 75 percent agreed that housing discrimination against gays ought to be against the law. Fifty-two percent believed that homosexuals ought to be able to inherit their partner's property and Social Security benefits. Yet only 33 percent supported the legalization of gay, or same-sex, marriage.

While the majority of Americans may not have been willing to accept families headed by two members of the same sex, the traditional nuclear family (father, mother, and their biological children) was no longer the standard in American society by the 1990s. Stepfamilies or blended families (father, mother, and biological or adopted children from a previous marriage or) represented the new American family. In 1999, there were already more than five-and-one-half million stepfamilies living in the United States.

Stepfamilies provided new living arrangements for divorced parents and adopted children, but many 1990s studies indicated that stepchildren were more likely to disobey authority, perform poorly in school, have to repeat a grade, or drop out of school. American children living in stepfamilies also were less likely to go to college or to receive financial support from their family if they did.

These studies provided ammunition for those Americans who supported "pro-family" social policies designed to discourage divorce and preserve the traditional nuclear family. Across the country, though, longstanding attitudes regarding stepfamilies began to change as men, women, and children who no longer identified with the traditional definitions of family sought ways to make their new families work. One example of the slowly growing acceptance of stepfamilies occurred in schools, as school officials began to acknowledge the increasingly important role of stepparents by accepting their signatures on school registration forms and field-trip permission slips.

For many Americans, the preferred vehicle of the 1990s was the Sports Utility Vehicle (SUV). Sales of SUVs doubled from 1990 to 1998, with more than three million sold in 1998 alone, making it one of the most popular vehicle types ever manufactured. SUVs are classified as a light truck. First introduced by Jeep more than two decades earlier, the SUV was originally designed for off-road driving and the towing of trailers and boats. Yet by the early 1990s, the vehicle became trendy as a family car, providing plenty of room for passengers and cargo. Like trucks and vans, SUVs also helped drivers to see over traffic, since they were built higher than a regular passenger car. To increase their popularity, designers made SUVs more comfortable, adding many coveted amenities such as CD stereo systems, cup holders, and leather interiors. By 1998, more than forty different models were available, including offerings from Ford (which produced the most popular model in the Ford Explorer), Jeep, Chevrolet, GMC, Nissan, and Toyota. Even luxury car manufacturers such as Mercedes Benz and Lexus marketed luxury SUV models for the discriminating driver.

❖ GUNS IN AMERICA

Shortly after the assassinations of Martin Luther King Jr. (April 4, 1968) and Robert F. Kennedy (June 5, 1968), the U.S. Congress passed the Gun Control Act of 1968. For more than twenty years this legislation defined federal gun policy. It banned most interstate sales of firearms, licensed most gun dealers, and barred felons, minors, and the mentally ill from purchasing and owning guns. Culturally, the law represented a brief national aversion to gun violence. In the 1990s, however, gun-control legislation became more quarrelsome and less extensive, and Americans witnessed a rash of mass shootings during the decade, many involving teenagers and children.

Although juvenile crime declined throughout the decade, the number of youths killed by gunfire increased an alarming 153 percent. Statistics suggested that one in twelve high school students was threatened or injured by a classmate with a gun every year. The growing sense among many Americans that no one was safe from unpredictable gun violence fueled the continuing debate over gun control.

According to a 1999 survey, 74 percent of Americans supported the registration of all handgun owners and 93 percent favored a mandatory waiting period for persons wishing to buy handguns. An additional 68 percent of those interviewed believed that military assault weapons ought to be outlawed, while 51 percent wanted to abolish gun shows at which weapons of all types can be bought and sold with little oversight. While estimates suggested that Americans still owned more than 235 million guns, the percentage of American households in which guns were present had declined slightly from the beginning of the decade.

Despite these statistics showing that most Americans wanted some type of gun control, the federal government was slow to act if it acted at all. Throughout the 1990s, political parties established gun control policy positions on in their platforms, politicians campaigned vigorously on different sides of the issue, and interest groups lobbied Congress and the courts to increase or reduce restrictions on firearms ownership. The controversy centered around the need to curb crime on one hand, and the Second Amendment to the U.S. Constitution (which gave citizens the right to bear arms) on the other. Pro-gun-control advocates claimed that some sort of gun control was necessary to maintain public order. Anti-gun-control proponents argued that law-abiding citizens had the constitutional right to use firearms to protect themselves and their property.

Understanding the public's concern over gun violence and drug-related crime, Democratic President Bill Clinton (1946–) worked with the Republican majority in Congress to pass groundbreaking crime-control legislation. Requiring background checks for handgun purchases had been debated in Congress since the attempted assassination of President Ronald Reagan (1911–) on March 30, 1981, but there was not enough support for passage of stricter gun controls. In 1994, however, amid a flurry of public controversy and media coverage, the Brady bill became law. The bill was named for Sarah Brady, antigun lobbyist and wife of James Brady—President Reagan's press secretary who had been severely injured by a bullet fired from a handgun during the failed assassination attempt on the president. The Brady Handgun Violence Prevention Act (Brady Law) was signed into law on November 30, 1993 and went into effect on February 28, 1994

The Brady Law established a national five-business-day waiting period (a "cooling off" period) for new gun purchases and required local law enforcement to conduct background checks on potential handgun buyers. The waiting period applied only to handgun sales through licensed dealers. Transfers between private individuals, as well as sales at gun shows and over the Internet, were excluded. The law required a licensed dealer to provide information from the purchaser's application to the chief law enforcement officer where the purchaser resides within one day of the proposed sale. This application, verified by some form of photo identification,

Road Rage

Incivility and rudeness seemed to penetrate every aspect of American life during the 1990s. This was no more evident than on the road, where American drivers became less considerate and more dangerous than ever before. By 1998, aggressive driving incidents—in which an angry or impatient driver tries to hurt or in some cases even kill another driver—had risen by 51 percent since the beginning of the decade. In several cases studied, 37 percent of those drivers used firearms against other drivers, 28 percent used other weapons, and 35 percent used their cars. Many motorists feared becoming a victim "road rage" more than being hit by a drunk driver. The phenomenon has since given rise to many books, articles, and special therapies that deal specifically with the problem. Studies have shown that increased traffic and longer commutes pave the way for shorter tempers and in some cases aggressive and dangerous behavior. Other factors that have contributed to the problem are the increasing popularity of trucks and SUVs, which, because of their height and weight, give a driver a greater feeling of power and invincibility than regular-sized automobiles.

must include the purchaser's name, address, date of birth, and the date it was completed. Local officials were then required to conduct a background check. The law also made the theft of a gun from a federal firearms licensee a federal crime punishable by a fine of up to ten thousand dollars and imprisonment up to ten years.

Another gun-control effort that succeeded in the 1990s was the Violent Crime Control and Law Enforcement Act (Assault Weapons Ban), which was passed by Congress in 1994. It made illegal the sale of nineteen specific types of semiautomatic weapons (those that reload automatically after firing). Though many other types of rifles, shotguns, and handguns are also semiautomatics, they were not included in the ban. At the time the law was passed, there were between one and two million semiautomatic assault weapons in circulation in the United States. The bill also banned copies or duplicates of the illegal weapons.

While gun control measures received support from many law enforcement agencies, as well as Democrats in Congress and large segments of the public, these efforts were strongly opposed by many firearms enthusiasts, interest groups, and Second Amendment supporters. One of the most vocal opponents of the restrictions was the National Rifle Association (NRA), which opposed the Brady Law, the Assault Weapons Ban, mandatory waiting periods, and restrictions on the manufacture, importation, and sale of any type of firearm, including semiautomatic assault weapons. The NRA claimed that such laws infringe on the right to bear arms as stated in the Second Amendment. Moreover, the organization contended that gun-control measures fail to keep career criminals from purchasing guns because they do not acquire them through licensed dealers, but from private individuals or through theft.

❖ THE NEW SPIRITUALISM

The New Age movement of the 1980s was not so much a religion as a blend of several Eastern philosophies. It also combined elements of Native American shamanism, early Christianity, and the counterculture of the 1960s. The movement avoided specific religious beliefs, teaching instead the ideas of individuality, oneness with nature, and simple lifestyles. Surveys in the 1980s estimated that 80 percent of Americans were affected by some form of spiritualism offered by the New Age movement.

In the 1990s, the New Age spiritualist movement continued to evolve. Whereas New Age in the 1980s often dealt with otherworldly notions such as reincarnation, out-of-body experiences, and the supernatural or extraterrestrial, New Age in the 1990s focused on self-fulfillment and personal happiness. In the process, the movement and its ideas became highly visible in mainstream America. The number of New Age bookstores in the United States during the decade exceeded five thousand, and millions of New Age books, audiotapes, and videos were sold. New Age authors such as Deepak Chopra and Marianne Williamson published best-sellers, became spiritual advisors to celebrities, and appeared on television shows such as *Oprah*.

The embracing of the newly transformed New Age spiritualism by Americans was no more evident than in the workplace. Increasingly during the 1990s, the phenomenon of "corporate spiritualism" came to be introduced as a means of motivating employees by emphasizing their independence and responsibility. Indebted to the New Age movement, advocates of corporate spiritualism asserted that the success or failure of workers depends solely on their individual imagination and initiative. Organizational factors should not hinder personal achievement, productivity, or fulfillment. Corporate spirituality, experts contended, should instead enhance a worker's intuition, energy, commitment, and productivity.

Following this idea, corporations tried to provide individuals with a medium through which to satisfy their needs and realize their goals, ideal-

From the boardroom to the bedroom and every living space in between, the principles of Feng Shui (pronounced fung SHWAY) became one of the interior-design industry's hottest trends during the 1990s. Feng Shui (meaning literally "wind water") is based on the ancient Chinese theory of organizing positive energy or "Ch'i" in living and working spaces. It seeks to create the most harmonious balance possible between the exterior environment and one's living or working space, as well as the personal energy of the individual. Translating Feng Shui into everyday applications, the serious practitioner studies a space to make sure that everything from the placement of furniture to the room color to the pictures or mirrors hanging on the walls is in balance with the forces of nature. Architects also studied the theory to determine the best placement and orientation for a building to maximize its positive energy. Homeowners solicited the help of Feng Shui practitioners and priests to decorate their homes and offices in order to avoid the pitfalls of financial ruin, bad luck, and tense family relations that could result from being out of balance with nature.

ly forming an alternate community and family. With enthusiasm and even love directed toward work, employees theoretically were supposed to transform what was once a chore into a tool to develop, nourish, and enrich their lives. In an effort to cement the link between employee self-fulfillment, job performance, and corporate profits, spiritual "inner-renewal" training programs gained momentum throughout the 1990s. A clear indication of the growing popularity of corporate spiritualism was the combined thirty billion dollars that American companies spent during the decade to promote it among their employees. The advocates of New Age corporate spiritualism thereby sought to foster employees's identification with a spiritualized corporate image, making work the means by which to achieve self-fulfillment and happiness.

❖ FASHION FOLLOWS MUSIC: THE GRUNGE AND HIP-HOP LOOK

Clothing trends for youth in the 1990s followed two music trends: grunge and hip-hop. Although the grunge look caught on quickly, it

Generation X

The roughly forty-five million children born between 1965 and 1980 made themselves heard during the 1990s. Known as Generation X (from the 1991 Douglas Coupland novel, *Generation X: Tales for an Accelerated Culture*), these youths were depicted at first as cynical, drifting, hopeless, and lazy. But this portrayal was far from accurate. Unlike the baby boomers (those born between 1946 and 1964), who tended to grow up in comfortable circumstances and who have come to accept prosperity as their due, Generation X never could rely on that kind of success. They grew up in the 1980s during a recession, witnessed increased divorce rates and the hard reality of homelessness, lived in the shadow of AIDS, and entered a job market that was tight and less rewarding. Despite these obstacles, Gen Xers have shown themselves to be hardworking, ambitious, and confident. They were the first group to have grown up with personal computers. By the end of the decade more than half of them had completed or enrolled in more than one year of college. Committed to a variety of social causes and also dedicated to making money, this group represented an impressive $125 billion in annual purchasing power.

peaked in the early part of the decade, then disappeared. Unlike grunge, hip-hop style not only lasted throughout the 1990s but was adopted by youth of all ages and races.

A new fashion scene took shape in 1991 when the Seattle-based alternative rock band Nirvana released its commercial breakthrough album, *Nevermind*. Suddenly, the Seattle music scene and its image was embraced by Generation X (as teens and young adults were sometimes called). The music tapped into the sense of anxiety shared by many young people as the economy continued to spiral downward early in the decade. Grunge was a backlash to the power dressing and elitism of the 1980s. The look of rock bands such as Soundgarden, Pearl Jam, Alice in Chains, and Nirvana was emulated by youth around the country.

The new uniform was not only easy to assemble, it was cheap: vintage thrift-store clothes fit in perfectly. Loose-fitting pants, either old jeans or long shorts for both girls and guys, formed the basis of the look. Long-sleeved undershirts or ratty flannel shirts worn over T-shirts defined grunge. Torn corduroy jackets or old cardigan sweaters were

*D.J. Crew, Ludacris, and
Fabolous at the Youth
Foundation Hip-Hop
Image Awards Gala in
Miami Beach, Florida.*
**Reproduced by permission of
AP/Wide World Photos.**

optional. Converse high-top sneakers, boots, and heavy-soled shoes (particularly Doc Martens) were preferred footwear. Baseball caps topped off the look. Like most trends, grunge eventually gave way to new fads. The rage began to ebb when twenty-seven-year-old Kurt Cobain, lead singer of Nirvana, was found dead from an apparently self-inflicted gunshot wound in April 1994.

While alternative rock brought grunge to the forefront in the early 1990s, hip-hop music created its own fashion empire throughout the decade. Hip-hop and rap, terms that were almost interchangeable, traced their roots back to black street music of the 1970s. This music, as well as its accompanying culture and fashion, grew throughout the 1980s and exploded in the 1990s. In 1998, for example, rap outsold country music, which was formerly the top-selling format in the United States. Rap sold more than eighty-one million compact discs and tapes that year. The growth of this musical format brought with it an incredible demand for its fashion counterpart.

The hip-hop look was diverse and evolved over time as it was adopted by white youth. One of the most enduring images of hip-hop, however, was baggy pants worn around the hip to expose underwear waistbands bearing designer names. Other essentials included pricey sneakers (sometimes worn with laces untied), hooded sweatshirts (known as "hoodies" and often worn with the hoods covering the head), and flashes of jewelry (preferably gold or platinum).

Casual Dress or Dressing Down?

Uncommon in the early 1990s, "dressing down" at work—wearing casual clothing at the office—became very popular within just a few years. Employers and employees called the innovation casual day, casual Friday (the day of the week it would most often occur), or office casual. As casual days in corporate America became more common, everyone seemed to have lower expectations about dressing formally. Americans began to dress down not only on designated workdays, but all the time. Jeans and sneakers became acceptable attire to wear just about everywhere. Celebrities went out on the town in bike shorts and baseball caps, and supermodels sported T-shirts and jeans. Movie stars showed up for film premieres dressed in baggy sweaters and pants. Rock stars such as Kurt Cobain of the Seattle band Nirvana popularized torn jeans, untucked flannel shirts, and ratty T-shirts. Although young people latched onto the "grunge" look as their own, adults were not immune to its influences. Even President Bill Clinton stopped looking presidential, as photographers snapped photograph after photograph of him jogging in shorts and logo T-shirts.

While these items defined hip-hop fashions, the look progressed: jeans that were extremely baggy at the start of the decade were merely loose by its end. Baseball caps that used to be worn backward faced front again or at least to the side. They also soon shared the top spot with ski caps (known as "skullies"). Hoodies made way for loose-fitting hockey jerseys, polo shirts, ski jackets, and varsity jackets. Sneakers paved the way for hiking boots.

Brand names also played an important role in hip-hop fashions, as many styles prominently featured logos. Jeans and shirts bearing the Tommy Hilfiger label were hot commodities, as was designer Ralph Lauren's Polo logo. African American labels—FUBU (an acronym for the slogan For Us by Us), Naughty Gear, Phat Farm, Pure Playaz, UB Tuff, and Wu-Wear—were particularly important in the hip-hop culture. Musicians and rappers such as LL Cool J, Tupac Shakur, Puff Daddy (who would also introduce his own line of fashions, Sean John), and Lauryn Hill helped to set style standards.

BOOKS

Bly, Robert. *Iron John: A Book About Men*. New York: Addison-Wesley, 1990.

Chopra, Deepak. *Ageless Body, Timeless Mind: The Quantum Alternative to Growing Old*. New York: Harmony Books, 1993.

Collins, Terah Kathryn. *The Western Guide to Feng Shui: Room by Room*. Carlsbad, CA: Hay House, 1999.

Sadler, Kim Martin, ed. *Atonement: The Million Man March*. Cleveland, OH: Pilgrim Press, 1996.

Streissguth, Tom. *Gun Control: The Pros and Cons*. Berkeley Heights, NJ: Enslow Publishers, 2001.

Williamson, Marianne. *A Return to Love: Reflections on the Principles of a Course in Miracles*. New York: HarperCollins, 1992.

WEB SITES

Brady Campaign to Prevent Gun Violence. http://www.bradycampaign.org/index.asp (accessed on May 17, 2002).

CNN-Million Man March-October 16, 1995. http://www.cnn.com/US/9510/megamarch/march.html (accessed on May 17, 2002).

GunCite: Gun Control and Second Amendment Issues. http://www.guncite.com (accessed on May 17, 2002).

National Rifle Association-MyNRA. http://www.nra.org/ (accessed on May 17, 2002).

New Age Spirituality. http://www.religioustolerance.org/newage.htm (accessed on May 17, 2002).

On2: Hip-Hop style. http://www.pbs.org/newshour/infocus/fashion/hiphop.html (accessed on May 17, 2002).

Yesterdayland-Fashion from the 90s. http://www.yesterdayland.com/popopedia/shows/decades/fashion_1990s.php (accessed on May 17, 2002).

chapter six *Medicine and Health*

1990: February 5 Smoking is banned on all U.S. domestic flights lasting less than six hours.

1990: March 9 Antonia Novello becomes the first woman and the first Hispanic American U.S. Surgeon General.

1990: September 14 U.S. geneticist W. French Anderson performs the first gene therapy on a human, injecting engineered genes into a four-year-old child to repair her faulty immune system.

1991: April 19 President George H. W. Bush is hospitalized overnight with atrial fibrillation (abnormal heartbeat).

1991: November 7 Earvin "Magic" Johnson announces that he has contracted the human immunodeficiency virus (HIV) and retires from professional basketball.

1991: November 20 Jack Kevorkian's medical license is suspended in Michigan in hopes of preventing him from assisting in any more patient suicides.

1992: An American Academy of Pediatrics task force recommends that babies be placed on their backs to sleep, leading to a decrease in reported cases of sudden infant death syndrome (SIDS).

1992: June 15 Earvin Johnson III, son of Magic and Cookie Johnson, is born. Mother and child are both HIV negative.

1993: September 8 Joycelyn Elders becomes the first African American U.S. Surgeon General.

1993: October 27 Embryologist Jerry Hall of George Washington University reports the first cloning of a human embryo.

1993: October 27 President Bill Clinton's 1,342-page Health Plan is delivered to the U.S. Congress.

1994: November In an open letter to the American public, former president Ronald Reagan announces that he has Alzheimer's disease.

1994: December 15 The U.S. Food and Drug Administration (FDA) permits the first U.S. test of RU-486, an abortion-inducing pill, in Des Moines, Iowa.

1994: December 31 Joycelyn Elders is forced to resign as Surgeon General following her controversial remarks about sex education, abortion, and drugs.

1995: March The FDA approves the first U.S. vaccine to prevent chicken pox, a disease afflicting 3.7 million people each year.

1995: March 6 Olympic gold-medal diver Greg Louganis announces he is HIV positive in his autobiography, *Breaking the Surface*.

1995: June 12 Actor Christopher Reeve is hospitalized with a neck fracture, spinal injury, and paralysis after a horseback-riding accident.

1996: May 13 The FDA approves the first new antiobesity drug in twenty-three years. In August 1997, the FDA will rescind its approval of the drug after the death of several diet patients.

1996: May 14 Jack Kevorkian is acquitted in a Pontiac, Michigan, court of assisted suicide charges for the third time.

1996: November Massachusetts legislators pass the first state law to permit consumers unlimited access to basic background information about physicians, including medical malpractice data.

1997: January 1 David Da-i Ho is named "Man of the Year" by *Time* magazine for his AIDS research.

1997: August 18 In DeForest, Wisconsin, ABS Global Inc. announces the birth of Gene, the first bull calf cloned from fetal stem cells.

1998: August 19 Nushawn Williams, a twenty-year-old New York man, is indicted on charges of felony reckless endangerment and attempted assault for knowingly exposing a fifteen-year-old girl to HIV while having sexual intercourse.

1998: September 2 The FDA approves the Preven Emergency Contraceptive Kit, which includes high-dosage birth control pills that prevent pregnancy if taken up to seventy-two hours after sexual intercourse.

1999: March 26 Jack Kevorkian is found guilty of second-degree murder and the delivery of a controlled substance by a Michigan jury and is sentenced to serve ten to twenty-five years in prison.

1999: December 1 Scientists from the United States, Japan, and England announce completion of the first mapping of an entire human genome, part of the Human Genome Project.

1999: December 28 Rhode Island becomes the last state in the country to approve the use of prescription drugs as an alternative to surgical abortion.

✳ *Overview*

American medicine in the 1990s made great technological advances, but the federal government's failure to reform the country's health-care system prevented many Americans from reaping the benefits of those advances. During his first term in office, President Bill Clinton fulfilled his campaign promise to address health-care reform by appointing his wife, Hillary Rodham Clinton, to chair a commission to study the issue and propose sweeping changes. In the end, the commission's proposals pleased no one, the U.S. Congress refused to act, and millions of working but uninsured Americans continued to live in fear of a sickness or an injury that could leave them bankrupt.

Another group of individuals who faced the fear of bankruptcy were those who suffered from AIDS. The epidemic, first identified in the 1980s, continued throughout the 1990s, growing in the United States during the first part of the decade. With the development of new drugs, the death rate from the disease began to decrease as the lives of those newly infected with HIV (the virus that causes AIDS) were extended. AIDS no longer became an immediate death sentence, but the drug therapy that kept people alive was very expensive, and medical insurers and pharmaceutical companies refused to make price concessions.

The controversial issue of abortion that had pitted Americans against one another since the 1970s continued into the 1990s, taking a hostile turn. Some antiabortion groups advocated violent terrorist tactics, not only picketing abortion clinics across the country but also bombing them and setting them on fire. Some extreme abortion opponents even gunned down physicians and other clinic personnel on the street or in their homes. Many on both sides of the issue decried such violence, but the debate over the legal right of abortion in the country remained heated.

Rapid improvements in medical technology in the 1990s brought about such scientific breakthroughs as gene therapy and cloning. With the promise of improving lives, these advances also raised troubling ethical and legal questions. Few individuals maintained that human gene therapy should not be used, especially if it can cure genetic disorders. Some feared, however, that if scientists can cure those disorders, they can also design individuals in accordance with the cultural and intellectual fashion of the day. Other saw further abuse through cloning. At the heart of the issue was the idea of humans tampering with life in a way that could harm society, either morally or in a real physical sense. Scientists fully agreed that further research was needed in the fields of gene therapy and cloning.

Robert C. Atkins (1930–) Cardiologist Robert C. Atkins advocated ideas about diet and nutrition that were controversial but also wildly popular. After first publishing a best-selling diet book in 1972, Atkins returned to the best-seller lists again in 1996 with *Dr. Atkins' New Diet Revolution.* He promoted eating foods high in fat and protein instead of foods which are low in fat but high in carbohydrates and soluble fiber. Although many celebrities and others endorsed Atkins's diet plan, the medical establishment condemned it. *Photo reproduced by permission of AP/Wide World Photos.*

Joycelyn Elders (1933–) Joycelyn Elders became the first African American to serve as U.S. Surgeon General after President Bill Clinton nominated her for the position in 1993. Her outspoken, controversial views, such as legalizing drugs and providing a broad sex education for students, immediately embroiled her in controversy. In 1994, during World AIDS Day at the United Nations, she suggested encouraging masturbation as a way to prevent teenagers from engaging in other sexual activities. The next day Clinton requested and received Elders's resignation. *Photo reproduced by permission of AP/Wide World Photos.*

David Da-i Ho (1952–) David Da-i Ho altered the way in which scientists and physicians understood HIV and AIDS in the 1980s and 1990s. His research showed that HIV attacked the immune system immediately after the body was infected. In 1995, he began a daring experiment, administering powerful new drugs called protease inhibitors in combination with standard antiviral medications to treat patients infected with HIV. With this approach, Ho came close to eliminating the virus from the blood in the early stages of infection. Although not a cure, Ho's treatment brought hope to those suffering with HIV. *Photo reproduced by permission of AP/Wide World Photos.*

Jack Kevorkian (1928–) Jack Kevorkian—Dr. Death—strongly advocated the right-to-die and doctor-assisted-suicide. The retired pathologist performed his first assisted-suicide in 1989, and presided over forty-seven more after 1990. He was charged and later acquitted in three assisted suicides; a fourth court case ended in a mistrial. Finally, in 1999, Kevorkian was convicted of second-degree murder after a videotape, which he had released to the television newsmagazine *60 Minutes,* showed him administering a lethal injection to his terminally ill patient. Had Kevorkian hooked up the man to his suicide machine, as he had done in the past, he likely would have been acquitted again. *Photo reproduced by permission of AP/Wide World Photos.*

❖ UNHEALTHY HEALTH CARE

Health-care reform was one of the first and most contentious major-policy initiatives tackled by President Bill Clinton (1946–). Health care had first become a public policy issue for Americans after World War II (1939–45), when President Harry S Truman (1884–1972) advocated national health insurance. The American Medical Association (AMA; the nation's leading medical organization), however, vigorously opposed it. Finally, in 1965, the Social Security Act established Medicare and Medicaid, providing medical insurance for retired persons (Medicare) and for those on welfare (Medicaid).

Other Americans still had to pay for their own health care, either through employer-sponsored insurance plans or out of their own pockets. The working poor assumed the most risk under these conditions because they did not qualify for Medicaid and generally worked for employers who did not offer medical insurance. From the 1960s to the 1980s, health-care costs continued to rise rapidly because of economic trends and technological advances in medicine. By the 1990s, even employers with health-care benefits found it difficult to continue to provide the level of protection to which workers had become accustomed without raising employees' premiums or reducing their benefits.

Health maintenance organizations (HMOs; prepaid group health plans) sought to lower insurance costs by focusing on preventive care rather than corrective medicine. HMOs also sought to reduce medical costs by requiring certain procedures to be authorized in advance by insurance companies. Family doctors were replaced by larger groups of salaried physicians, which lowered overhead costs for the HMO but made health care less personal. Despite these cost controls attempted by the HMOs, health costs and insurance premiums continued to rise.

Calls for health-care reform came from across the nation, but lobbying from special-interest groups such as the AMA often got in the way. In 1991, more than three dozen health-care reform bills were introduced in the U.S. Congress. None of them passed. The following year, President George H. W. Bush presented a health-care reform plan that promised to provide coverage for the more than thirty-five million Americans without health insurance and to stop the spiraling costs for the Medicare system. This legislation, too, died in Congress.

Finally, in 1993, President Clinton responded to the health-care crisis by choosing First Lady Hillary Rodham Clinton, to lead efforts to reform

Doctors' Average Salaries in 1995

Specialty	Salary
Radiology	$230,000
General surgery	$225,000
Anesthesiology	$203,000
Obstetrics/Gynecology	$200,000
Pathology	$185,000
Emergency medicine	$170,000
Internal medicine	$138,000
Pediatrics	$129,000
Psychiatry	$124,000
Family practice	$124,000

the $900-billion American health-care system. In October of that year, President Clinton unveiled the plan developed by Mrs. Clinton's task force. The National Health Security Plan proposed to overhaul U.S. health care. All Americans would receive health insurance coverage under the plan. The plan would have been financed through a combination of savings in existing programs, new revenues, and a series of subsidies or grants. Employers would pay 80 percent of their employees' health insurance premiums, with the government providing subsidies to low-income workers and some small businesses. There would have been a seventy-five-cent per-pack cigarette tax. All insurance would be purchased through regional health alliances under government control. The plan also required half of U.S. medical school graduates to specialize in primary care.

Even before the plan reached Congress, the insurance industry, the Republican Party, the AMA, and other groups had organized a media campaign against it. They labeled the plan "socialized medicine" (a system of national health care regulated and subsidized by the government, such as those in Canada and Great Britain). They claimed the plan would reduce the quality of medical services in the country and remove a patient's right to choose his or her own doctor. The AARP (American Association of Retired Persons, the nation's largest organization for people over the age of fifty) had initially supported Clinton's plan. The influential lobbyist group switched sides, however, when its members began to fear that they would lose the option of being able to choose their own doctors and other health-care providers. Without a strong support system among the public, lawmakers were unwilling to jeopardize their political careers by supporting the controversial plan.

After being introduced into Congress, the National Health Security Plan was assigned to several committees that held hearings on it over the next year. Parts of the plan were eventually made into law, but in vastly different forms that hardly reformed anything. Most of the plan simply died in committee. Even President Clinton gave up supporting it, realizing it was a lost cause. Various Democrats and Republicans in Congress offered competing health-care reform plans throughout the 1990s. Some minor bills were passed, but most major reform efforts continued to stagnate. By the end of the decade, the U.S. medical system of private insurance and market-driven health care remained largely unchanged.

❖ AIDS: THE CONTINUING EPIDEMIC

Throughout the 1990s, the acquired immunodeficiency syndrome (AIDS) epidemic continued to take a devastating toll in human lives all over the globe. In 1999, 2.8 million people worldwide died from the disease, bringing the total number of deaths attributed to AIDS by the end of the twentieth century to 18.8 million. In 1999 alone, almost 5.5 million people worldwide were infected with the human immunodeficiency virus (HIV; the virus that causes AIDS)—roughly fifteen thousand new cases each day. In the United States, the reported number of Americans living with HIV/AIDS at the end of the decade was 412,471. The Centers for Disease Control and Prevention (CDC; the federal government agency responsible for developing and applying disease prevention and control) estimated the actual number was probably double that, since many cases went unreported.

President Bill Clinton looking on as his wife, Hillary, speaks about health care in the United States in 1993. Reproduced by permission of the Corbis Corporation.

In spite of these staggering numbers, death rates for those suffering from AIDS in the United States declined dramatically during the decade. AIDS fell from being the eighth-leading cause of death in 1996 to fourteenth a year later. Medical researchers and others attributed this decline

Gulf War Syndrome

About 697,000 men and women of the U.S. military served in the Persian Gulf War. The conflict began in August 1990 when Iraq invaded and occupied Kuwait and culminated in February 1991 with an armed battle between Iraq and a coalition of nations led by the United States. After the war ended, some U.S. service personnel returned home with various illnesses such as asthma, short-term memory loss, fatigue, rash, muscle aches and pains, and weakness. This collection of diverse symptoms affecting returning veterans became known as the Gulf War syndrome.

Despite receiving medical discharges, some veterans were denied full disability pay. The military and the Veterans Affairs Department initially dismissed the complaints as unrelated to service in the Persian Gulf. Spouses of some veterans came down with some of the symptoms as well, and some of their pregnancies resulted in premature births and an elevated incidence of birth defects and illnesses.

The potential causes of the syndrome are as varied as its symptoms. Soldiers breathed smoke from burning waste dumps and oil wells and encountered a variety of paints, solvents, and pesticides. Some veterans believe they were exposed to chemical or germ warfare agents that were dispersed into the air after the coalition bombed Iraqi storage facilities.

to the development of multidrug "cocktails," a potent combination of antiviral drugs often including protease (pronounced PRO-tee-aze inhibitors), which were first developed by drug researchers in 1994. Protease inhibitors, working in combination with other drugs, suppressed the spread of HIV in the cells of the person infected.

If a newly infected individual started this drug treatment soon after diagnosis, the patient could delay the onset of AIDS symptoms for many years. This delay allowed many HIV-positive men and women to enjoy relatively normal lives. Although AIDS remained incurable, it now was viewed as a chronic (long-term) condition rather than one that was immediately fatal. Unfortunately, this treatment regimen had two major drawbacks: Researchers found that once HIV-infected people stopped their drug therapy, the virus rebounded in their bodies. Also, the treatment was very expensive. This had significant implications for health insurance cov-

The U.S. military acknowledged that it had detected minute traces of sarin (a nerve agent) and mustard gas in the desert.

Another potential source of the problem may have been medications administered to the U.S. soldiers to protect them against chemical weapons. Researchers at Duke University and the University of Texas linked the veterans' problems to chemicals used to protect them from insects and nerve gas. Studies showed that animals treated with only one of the drugs in question did not develop illnesses, but those receiving both the antinerve-gas pill and the insect repellents did exhibit symptoms resembling Gulf War syndrome.

Between 1994 and the end of the decade, the U.S. Defense Department spent $100 million on Gulf War health research. In 1999, a report prepared for the Defense Department pointed out that the drug administered to protect the soldiers against chemical weapons could not be ruled out as a possible cause of the syndrome. While no definitive answer was determined as to the cause of illness, the Department of Veterans Affairs and the Department of Defense now recognize that the Gulf War syndrome is a real medical condition.

erage and hospital costs. Many AIDS patients exhausted the coverage limits permitted by their insurers and were forced to deplete their life savings to pay for the vital and necessary drug therapy.

Battling AIDS has been a political as well as a scientific fight ever since the disease was first reported in 1981. Robert C. Gallo of the Tumor Cell Biology Laboratory of the National Cancer Institute in the United States and his French rival, Luc Montagnier of the Pasteur Institute in France, both claimed to have been the first to isolate and identify the HIV virus. More was at stake than pride, however, since the claim determined control over patent rights for increasingly important diagnostic tests. Other issues in the debate were hotly contested. Since AIDS was often perceived as being transmitted by homosexual activity and intravenous drug use, some members of the religious community argued that the disease represented divine punishment for immoral behavior. Uncomfortable with the link

Top Causes of Death in America in 1995

Cause	Number
1) Heart disease	737,563
2) Cancer	538,455
3) Stroke	157,991
4) Lung disease	102,899
5) Accidents	93,320
6) Influenza and pneumonia	82,923
7) Diabetes	59,254
8) HIV/AIDS	43,115
9) Suicide	31,284
10) Liver disease	25,222

between AIDS and homosexual behavior, President Ronald Reagan (1911–) and his administration hardly addressed the issue in the 1980s.

The homosexual community and others pressured pharmaceutical companies and the government throughout the 1990s to increase spending on AIDS research, treatment, and prevention. Although effective in prolonging life, anti-AIDS drugs were expensive; their manufacturers faced criticism for profiting from the suffering of desperately sick people. Pharmaceutical companies also were attacked for not supplying the drugs at reduced cost to impoverished areas of the world where the disease was rampant, such as Africa. Activists also accused the U.S. Food and Drug Administration (FDA) of being too slow to approve some new anti-AIDS drugs and for approving other drugs too hastily without assuring their safety and effectiveness.

Because AIDS was most often transmitted through unprotected sexual relations and had long been associated with homosexual activity, many people sought to hide their HIV status. In fact, a few infected individuals were prosecuted for not telling their partners of their HIV status before engaging in unprotected sex. On several occasions, individuals were charged with having used the HIV virus as a lethal weapon by intentionally infecting others with the disease.

Perhaps because the disease struck hard within the arts community, playwrights and filmmakers took up the cause against AIDS in the 1990s.

OPPOSITE PAGE
The AIDS memorial quilt on display in Washington, D.C., in 1996. Started in 1987, the quilt has served as a memorial for those who have died of AIDS, while also serving to educate others about the disease. Reproduced by permission of Paul Margolies.

Early in the decade, Tony Kushner's play *Angels in America,* winner of four Tony Awards and the 1993 Pulitzer Prize for drama, focused on AIDS. In film, Tom Hanks gave an Academy Award-winning performance as an AIDS-infected lawyer fighting to keep his job in *Philadelphia* (1993). The acclaimed made-for-television movie, *And The Band Played On* (1993), told the story of the discovery of AIDS. Almost everyone who attended the Academy Awards ceremonies during the 1990s wore a small red ribbon, demonstrating their commitment to curing AIDS and their compassion for its victims.

Although the search for an AIDS cure vaccine continued throughout the 1990s, progress was painfully slow. Like the virus that causes the common cold, HIV tends to mutate readily. A vaccine or cure for one strain proved to be worthless against other mutated forms. The only known ways to prevent the spread of the disease—abstinence (complete avoidance) from both unprotected sex and from sharing intravenous drug needles—demanded changes in patterns of social behavior. Unfortunately, unsafe sexual practices—including sex among teenagers—were again on the upswing in America at the close of the decade.

❖ ABORTION: THE CONTINUING FIGHT

Abortion continued to divide the nation as it had since the 1973 *Roe* v. *Wade* decision by the U.S. Supreme Court, which established a woman's legal right to choose an abortion during the first trimester of pregnancy. Throughout the 1980s, debates between antiabortionists (often called pro-life advocates) and those who supported a woman's right to choose (often called pro-choice advocates) grew increasingly heated. In the late 1980s, Operation Rescue, a zealous antiabortion group, inspired and encouraged a nationwide militant antiabortion movement that aggressively protested at clinics where abortions were performed.

While street protests in front of clinics continued in the 1990s, a few antiabortion advocates adopted terrorist tactics, murdering doctors who provided abortion services in Florida and New York. On March 10, 1993, antiabortionist Michael Frederick Griffin gunned down physician David Gunn at the entrance to a Pensacola, Florida abortion clinic. Griffin was convicted of murder and sentenced to life in prison. The following year, on July 29, 1994, John Bayard Britton, a physician who performed abortions, and his escort, James H. Barnett, were murdered in Pensacola by Paul Jennings Hill, a former Presbyterian minister. In 1994 alone there were twelve attempted or actual murders of abortion clinic personnel, as well as twelve additional attacks on clinics by bombs or fire. On October 23, 1998, while he sat in the kitchen of his home outside Buffalo, New York, Barnett Slepi-

*Demonstrators from the
pro-life group Operation
Rescue at a sit-in in
Buffalo, New York, in
1992. Reproduced by
permission of AP/Wide
World Photos.*

an, a doctor who performed abortions, was shot and killed by a sniper. At
the end of the decade, Slepian's killer remained at large.

Slepian's name, along with those of hundreds of other physicians,
judges, and prominent feminists across the United States, had appeared on
an Internet Web site known as the "Nuremberg Files." (The name is in reference to the war crimes trial held at Nuremberg, Germany, after World
War II [1939–45]). Besides names, the Web site listed photographs, home
and work addresses, phone numbers, and other personal information.

When an individual on the list was injured in an attack, his or her name was grayed out; when an individual was killed, his or her name was marked with a strike through it. Spokespersons for both Planned Parenthood and the National Abortion Federation considered the sponsors of the site responsible for antiabortion violence. On February 2, 1999, a federal court agreed and ordered the Web site shut down.

The introduction of prescription drugs to help induce abortion soon changed the landscape surrounding the contentious and violent issue. Drugs such as methotrexate, an anticancer medication, were successfully used to terminate pregnancies. Oral contraceptives taken in high doses also were effective in terminating pregnancies more than 75 percent of the time. The first major alternative to surgical abortion, however, was the prescription drug mefipristone or RU-486. First developed in 1980 in France and approved for use in 1988, RU-486 had helped induce abortions in more than six hundred thousand women in countries across Europe by 1999. Yet RU-486 was not available to American women, primarily because manufacturers, afraid of boycotts, chose not to distribute the drug in America until the early 1990s. Clinical trials of the drug were finally conducted in the United States beginning in 1994. Finding it safe and effective, the U.S. Food and Drug Administration (FDA) approved the marketing of RU-486 in 2000.

❖ GENE THERAPY AND CLONING: A POSSIBLE FUTURE

Genetic information in humans is stored in units known as genes, which carry instructions for the formation, functioning, and transmission of specific traits from one generation to the next. Genes determine individual human characteristics—from eye and hair color to height to musical and literary talent. In 1953, English chemist Francis Crick (1916–) and American biologist James Watson (1928–) first determined the chemical explanation for a gene. They discovered the chemical structure for deoxyribonucleic acid (DNA; large, complex molecules that occur in the nuclei of all living cells and are unique to each person). Genes make up the segments of DNA.

Genetic disorders are conditions that originate in an individual's genetic make-up. Many of these disorders are inherited and are governed by the same rules that determine whether a person has dimples or red hair. Medical scientists know of about three thousand disorders that arise from errors in an individual's DNA. Conditions such as sickle-cell anemia, muscular dystrophy, and cystic fibrosis result from the loss, mistaken insertion, or change of a gene in a DNA molecule. For years, scientists have sought to find a way to correct these deficient genes—a procedure known as human gene therapy (HGT).

Alone in Antarctica: Physician Heal Thyself

The National Science Foundation's Amundsen-Scott South Pole Station is located at the geographic South Pole in Antarctica. Composed of a number of structures, the station houses instruments used to monitor the upper and lower atmosphere and to conduct astronomy and astrophysics research. The station's winter personnel, some twenty-eight scientists and support crew, are isolated between mid-February and late October. Temperatures in mid-winter drop to one hundred degrees Fahrenheit below zero.

In March 1999, the only doctor at the station, forty-seven-year-old Jerri Nielsen, discovered a lump in her right breast. In June, after telling the rest of the crew at the station about her condition, she began corresponding with a breast cancer specialist at Indiana University via e-mail. Because of the severe winter weather, Nielsen could not be evacuated from the station. She and her colleagues at the station would have to perform the necessary diagnostic operation to determine if the lump were cancerous.

On July 11, in a dangerous and challenging mission, an Air Force C-141 Starlifter made a fifteen-hour round-trip flight from New Zealand and air-dropped medical supplies for diagnosis and treatment, including chemotherapy drugs. Nielsen then directed a few crew members through the procedure of removing lump tissue from her affected breast. Digital microscopic images of the lump cells were then transmitted by video back to the cancer specialist in the United States. The specialist confirmed Nielsen's diagnosis of breast cancer, and the crew began to give her the chemotherapy drugs.

Although the tumor shrank at first, it soon began to grow. Nielsen's doctor urged that she be evacuated from the station as soon as possible. Along with another ailing member of the crew, she agreed to the daring rescue mission. On October 16, 1999, after several missions were delayed because of weather, a U.S. National Guard crew landed, picked up the pair, and dropped off a replacement physician. Back in the United States, Nielsen eventually underwent a mastectomy (surgical removal of her breast).

In May 1990, a research team at the National Institutes of Health (NIH) attempted HGT on a four-year-old girl suffering from a rare immune deficiency. The patient received about one billion cells containing a genetically engineered copy of the gene that her body lacked. In 1993,

Breast Implants

Silicone gel implants—used to cosmetically enhance women's breasts—were developed in 1964. By the late 1990s, between 1.5 and 1.8 million American women had undergone breast implant surgery. Because these implants were developed prior to a 1976 law requiring Food and Drug Administration (FDA) approval, they did not have to undergo federal scientific testing. Women and their doctors assumed breast implants were safe. In May 1992, however, the FDA finally conducted hearings to determine implants' safety.

The FDA panel found that the implants had not been proven to be safe, but neither was there conclusive evidence that they were harmful. In April 1993, the FDA temporarily banned using silicone gel implants for cosmetic purposes while studies continued. Despite the inconclusive evidence and the ongoing research, the implant crisis soon made national headlines. Patients with complaints or problems they felt were caused by their breast implants appeared on magazine covers and on television talk shows. They also began to file lawsuits against implant makers.

Mounting scientific evidence that the implants did not cause cancer or other diseases did little to influence judges or juries. As a result, multimillion-dollar verdicts were returned against the implant manufacturers. The largest manufacturer, Dow Corning, decided to cut its losses and stopped making implants. Ultimately, Dow Corning agreed to settle the pending lawsuits in order to end the legal proceedings.

the NIH approved a procedure to introduce normal genes into the airways of cystic fibrosis patients. According to the NIH, by 1999 more than 390 gene therapy studies had been initiated, involving over four thousand people and more than a dozen medical conditions.

Despite such successes, most HGT experiments have produced largely disappointing results. In 1999, HGT research was dealt a severe blow when Jesse Gelsinger, an eighteen-year-old from Tucson, Arizona, died in an experiment at the University of Pennsylvania. The young man, who suffered from a rare genetic liver disorder, had volunteered for an experiment to test gene therapy for babies with a fatal form of that disease. His death led to demands for increased oversight of HGT research and forced researchers to defend their program publicly.

American Nobel Prize Winners
in Physiology or Medicine

Year	Scientist
1990	Joseph E. Murray E. Donnall Thomas
1991	No award given to an American
1992	Edmond H. Fischer Edwin G. Krebs
1993	Phillip A. Sharp
1994	Alfred G. Gilman Martin Rodbell
1995	Edward B. Lewis Eric F. Wieschaus
1996	No award given to an American
1997	Stanley B. Prusiner
1998	Robert F. Furchgott Louis J. Ignarro Ferid Murad
1999	Günter Blobel

A scientific breakthrough in the 1990s was cloning even more startling than gene therapy. Cloning is the creation of a cell, group of cells, or an entire organism that contains the same genetic information as that of the parent cell or organism. Humans have utilized simple methods of plant cloning such as grafting and stem cutting for more than two thousand years. The first cloning of animal cells took place in 1964, and the first successful cloning of mammals was achieved nearly twenty years later. These experiments had one characteristic in common: They involved the use of embryonic cells, those at a very early stage of development. Biologists have always believed that such cells have the ability to adapt to new environments and are able to grow and develop in a cell other than the one from which they are taken. Adult cells, they thought, did not retain the same adaptability.

A startling announcement in February 1997 showed an error in this line of reasoning. A team of Scottish researchers, led by embryologist Ian Wilmut (1945–), reported that they had cloned an adult mammal for the first time. The product of the experiment was a sheep named Dolly, seven months old at the time of the announcement. She differed from previous cloning experiences in that she originated from an adult cell. A study of Dolly's genetic make-up showed that she was identical to the adult female sheep that supplied genetic material for the experiment.

Advances in the cloning process developed rapidly after Dolly's debut. Only a year and half later, biologists from the University of Hawaii announced in July 1998 they had cloned dozens of mice—even cloning some of the clones. What made the cloning of adult mice astounding is that mouse embryos develop soon after being fertilized. Due to this speedy embryonic development, scientists had thought a mouse would prove to be difficult or impossible to clone..

When scientists and others suggested the possibility of cloning humans, an active debate arose in the country about the morality of such an undertaking. In March 1997, President Bill Clinton (1946–) banned research into human cloning in all federally sponsored laboratories and asked that private researchers also comply with the ban. In January 1998, however, physicist Richard Seed announced his intention to attempt human cloning. Research into animal cloning continued. Despite the controversy and potential limitations, scientists argued that cloning could benefit society by preserving endangered species and advancing medical understanding of aging and diseases.

 For More Information

BOOKS

Atkins, Robert C. *Dr. Atkins' New Diet Revolution.* Revised and updated ed. New York: M. Evans, 1999.

Elders, Joycelyn, and David Chanoff. *Joycelyn Elders, M.D.: From Sharecropper's Daughter to Surgeon General of the United States of America.* New York: Morrow, 1996.

Kolata, Gina. *Clone: The Road to Dolly, and the Path Ahead.* New York: Morrow, 1998.

Nielsen, Jerri, with Maryanne Vollers. *Ice Bound: A Doctor's Incredible Battle for Survival at the South Pole.* New York: Talk Miramax Books, 2001.

White, Katherine. *Everything You Need to Know About AIDS and HIV.* New York: Rosen Publishing Group, 2001.

WEB SITES

AIDS History Center. http://www.aidshistory.org/aidshist.htm (accessed on May 21, 2002).

AIDS.ORG-Quality Treatment Information and Resources. http://www.aids.org/index.html (accessed on May 21, 2002).

CDC-NCHSTP-Divisions of HIV/AIDS Prevention (DHAP) Home Page. http://www.cdc.gov/hiv/dhap.htm (accessed on May 21, 2002).

Cloning Fact Sheet. http://www.ornl.gov/hgmis/elsi/cloning.html (accessed on May 21, 2002).

Gene Therapy. http://www.ornl.gov/hgmis/medicine/genetherapy.html (accessed on May 21, 2002).

National Health Security Plan. http://www.ibiblio.org/nhs/NHS-T-o-C.html (accessed on May 21, 2002).

Nobel e-Museum. http://www.nobel.se/index.html (accessed on May 21, 2002).

Science and Technology

1990: **April 24** The Hubble Space Telescope is placed into orbit by the space shuttle *Discovery*.

1990: **October 1** The Human Genome Project (HGP) is formally launched.

1991: Linus Torvalds, a student at the University of Helsinki (Finland), writes the code for the open-source Linux operating system and releases it over the Internet under a free public license.

1991: **September 26** Four men and four women begin a two-year stay inside a sealed-off structure in Oracle, Arizona, called Biosphere 2.

1992: **May 7 to 16** During a space shuttle mission, three astronauts from the *Endeavor* simultaneously walk in space for the first time, retrieving and repairing the Intelsat-6 satellite; their walk lasts eight hours and twenty-nine minutes.

1992: **June 9** The largest-ever environmental summit, known as the Earth Summit, opens in Rio de Janeiro, Brazil, with participants from 178 nations.

1993: An international research team in Paris, France, produces a rough gene map of all twenty-three pair of human chromosomes.

1993: **September 6** The "Doomsday 2000" article, warning about possible Y2K (Year 2000) computer problems, is published in *Computerworld* by Canadian Peter de Jager.

1994: Scientists discover three planets orbiting the dim remnants of a star that exploded long ago, evidence of a solar system beyond our own.

1994: **December 15** Netscape Communications Corporation releases its graphical World Wide Web browser, Netscape Navigator 1.0, initiating a communications revolution. Within four months, 75 percent of all Internet users are accessing the Web using this browser.

1995: J. Craig Venter and Hamilton Smith publish a paper in *Science* announcing they have successfully mapped the entire genome of *Haemophilus influenzae,* a bacterium that causes ear infections and meningitis.

1995: **January 2** The most distant galaxy yet observed is found by scientists using the Keck telescope at the W. M. Keck Observatory in Mauna Kea, Hawaii. The galaxy is estimated to be fifteen billion light-years away from Earth.

1995: **August** A group of schoolchildren on a biology class field trip in Minnesota discover deformed frogs, leading to a national fear that pesticides, toxins, and global warming are wreaking havoc on the environment.

1996: The first U.S. Congressional hearing on the Y2K problem is held, focusing on how federal agencies will prepare their computer systems for the year 2000.

1996: The first genetically engineered insect, a predator mite that researchers hope will eat other mites that damage strawberries and other crops, is released in Florida.

1996: September 25 NASA biochemist Shannon Lucid returns home after spending six months aboard the Russian space station *Mir,* earning her the title of America's most experienced astronaut.

1997: April 21 The ashes of 1960s LSD guru Timothy Leary and *Star Trek* creator Gene Roddenberry are blasted into space in the first space funeral.

1997: June 26 The U.S. Supreme Court determines that the Communications Decency Act, meant to regulate "indecent" material on the Internet, is unconstitutional.

1997: December Representatives from 160 countries meet in Kyoto, Japan, to discuss climate change and draft the Kyoto Protocol, an agreement effective by the year 2012, which restricts greenhouse gas emissions associated with global warming.

1998: J. Craig Venter and his private research company Celera Genomics announce plans to decode the entire human genome by 2001, years ahead of the government-sponsored Human Genome Project deadline.

1998: February 21.74 inches of rain fall on Santa Barbara, California—its highest monthly total on record. Scientists speculate that this deluge is the result of weather changes caused by global warming.

1998: October 29 The space shuttle *Discovery* launches with seventy-seven-year-old U.S. senator and former astronaut John Glenn aboard as a payload specialist.

1999: April 30 *Science* publishes two companion articles indicating that the deformities of the frogs found in Minnesota and other states are primarily caused by a parasite, not by global warming or pesticides as was previously theorized.

1999: November/December In the world of e-commerce, online holiday sales tripled from a total of $73 million in 1998 to more than $3 billion.

Overview

As the twentieth century drew to a close, the potential for human invention and understanding appeared boundless. Scientific discoveries expanded daily, from the fundamental building blocks of matter to the source code of all life to the origins (and perhaps the eventual end) of the universe. Optimism was the reigning tone of the decade. New advances in science and technology seemed to promise solutions to problems ranging from eliminating toxic waste to grocery shopping.

The Human Genome Project, launched in 1990 with a mission to decode the entire human genetic makeup, held out the promise that the source of genetic diseases could be discovered and the diseases subsequently cured. However, many people worried about what scientists might do with a complete understanding of the human genetic code. Some feared this information might be used to discriminate against people susceptible to certain genetic malfunctions or to group individuals based on their genetic data. The idea that private companies were competing to win patents on genetic discoveries was disturbing as well. Nevertheless, most Americans supported this research that could ultimately provide information to make lives better.

With the creation of the Internet and the World Wide Web, many individuals found that greater access to information increased their sense of personal freedom and power. It gave birth to a new society of technologically connected citizens with a world of digitized information, commerce, and communication at their fingertips. The "Information Superhighway," however, was not open to all. Some Americans, including older citizens and those who could not afford the new technology, lacked access.

Still, by 1999 more than three-quarters of the U.S. population was "plugged in" to the new digital society.

The National Aeronautics and Space Administration (NASA) continued to amaze the world in the 1990s, despite mishaps and miscalculations. It sent the giant Hubble Space Telescope into orbit to gather and transmit never-before-seen images of deep space that offered increasingly tantalizing clues to the origins of the universe. It found possible evidence of bacterial life in a meteor from Mars and discovered distant planets that might contain water. NASA also sent space probes to land on the surface of Mars and made plans to build an International Space Station with research teams from other countries.

Still, some critics wondered if all of the money spent on space research might not be better used to fund new discoveries here on Earth, especially ones that could help correct environmental problems. Scientists studying the climate on Earth became increasingly concerned during the decade that average temperatures around the planet were rising, mainly due to the burning of fossil fuels, which release carbon dioxide. As the atmosphere becomes filled with more and more carbon dioxide, it traps more and more heat that should normally escape into space. A continual rise in temperature could have disastrous effects on the world. One result might be the melting of Earth's ice caps at the North and South Poles, with a resulting increase in the volume of the oceans' water. Were that to happen, many of the world's largest cities—those located along the edge of the oceans—might be flooded. Conferences addressing such problems were held around the world in the 1990s, with representatives from hundred of countries attending. Unfortunately, the ongoing debate about the environment and humans' effect on it remained just that, as environmental activists and those with a more conservative outlook failed to reach any meaningful agreements.

Marc Andreessen (1971–) Marc Andreessen, a student working at the National Center for Superconducting Applications, created an easy-to-use, point-and-click graphical interface browser called Mosaic for the World Wide Web in 1993. (A browser is a computer program that retrieves and interprets documents on the Web.) Mosaic permitted users to click on icons (pictures of symbols) and view pictures, listen to audio, and see video. Realizing the browser needed to continually evolve, Andreessen formed his own company, Netscape Communications. In 1994, the company released its browser, Netscape Navigator, which became an overnight success. *Photo reproduced by permission of Netscape Communications, Inc.*

Tim Berners-Lee (1955–) Tim Berners-Lee wrote a relatively easy-to-learn coding system called HyperText Markup Language (HTML) as a way to open his computer to other computers, allowing users to link their documents with his. In 1989, he proposed expanding this system into a global hypertext project known as the World Wide Web that would allow users anywhere to view nearly any document on the Internet. He also designed an addressing scheme that gave each Web page a unique location, or universal resource locator (URL). The World Wide Web debuted in 1991, making the Internet useful and available to the world. *Photo reproduced by permission of AP/Wide World Photos.*

Shannon Lucid (1943–) Astronaut Shannon Lucid flew on five space flights during her career, the most any woman has undertaken. On March 23, 1996, she blasted off in the space shuttle *Atlantis,* bound for the Russian *Mir* space station. She remained on the space station for 188 days and 4 hours, traveling 75.2 million miles. It was the longest period of time ever spent in space by a U.S. astronaut. Afterward, Lucid received the Congressional Space Medal of Honor, the first and only woman to be so honored. *Photo reproduced by permission of AP/Wide World Photos.*

J. Craig Venter (1946–) J. Craig Venter in 1995 helped map the entire genome (complete genetic information of an organism) of a bacterium that caused ear infections and meningitis. This was the first time the genetic secrets of an entire living organism had been exposed. By the end of the decade, a total of twenty genomes had been fully decoded worldwide, ten of them at his research facility. In 1998, Venter and others teamed up to form a new corporation called Celera Genomics. The company proposed to finish a map of the estimated three-billion-letter human genome by 2001. *Photo reproduced by permission of AP/Wide World Photos.*

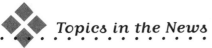

❖ HUMAN GENOME PROJECT

The Human Genome Project (HGP), officially launched on October 1, 1990, is a multibillion-dollar, international scientific research effort to map all of the estimated fifty to one hundred thousand genes on the twenty-three pairs of human chromosomes and read their entire sequence or arranged order. In the center of any normal human cell, there are forty-six X-shaped chromosomes (twenty-three pairs), and within each chromosome is bundled a long, coiled molecule called deoxyribonucleic acid (DNA). Each DNA molecule contains identifiable subunits known as genes. Each gene carries genetic instructions for everything from hair color and height to how the brain is organized. All of the genes together are called the genome. Thus mapping or decoding all of the genes in the human genome would give scientists unprecedented understanding of the human body and could point to the eventual diagnosis, cure, or elimination of many genetic diseases or disorders.

The HGP is a mammoth, thirteen-year federal project involving scientists from at least eighteen countries. In 1998, a private company, Celera Genomics, entered into the research. Francis S. Collins, director of the National Human Genome Research Institute (NHGRI) at the National Institutes of Health (NIH), asserted that this research is the most important organized scientific effort that humankind has ever attempted. By 1999, one-quarter of the human genome code had been spelled out by teams of government-sponsored scientists and by their corporate competitors. Computer technology played an important role in making genetic research possible. It provided the communication and organizational medium to manage the genetic information that was discovered, and provided the tools to create machines that made it easier to sequence genes.

In December 1999, an international team announced it had achieved a scientific milestone by compiling nearly the entire code of a human chromosome for the first time. Researchers chose chromosome twenty-two because of its relatively small size (just over thirty-three million pieces or chemical components) and its link to many major diseases. The sequence they compiled is over twenty-three million letters in length and is the longest continuous stretch of DNA ever deciphered and assembled. Researchers were able to find only 97 percent of the genetic material, but the results were considered complete for the time. More than thirty human disorders already were associated with changes to the genes of this chromosome, including a form of leukemia, disorders of fetal development and the nervous system, and schizophrenia. Scientists expected the decoding of the rest of the genome to come quickly.

Private companies that were working to map the human genome hoped to beat the HGP to the finish line in order to win lucrative patents on new genetic discoveries. J. Craig Venter, president of Celera Genomics Corporation, declared in 1998 that his company would have a map of the entire human genome ready in 2001, years ahead of the original HGP estimated date of completion of 2005. His announcement forced the leaders of the HGP to move up their deadline to 2003 for a finished product and 2001 for a "working draft."

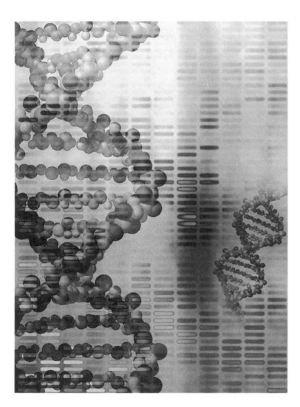

Critics of Venter and other private researchers argued that racing to decode the entire human genome would make for sloppy and incomplete results, but private companies asserted that the painstakingly precise research done at the HGP was slow and unnecessary. They argued that mapping all of the genes in encyclopedic detail delayed scientists from finding and concentrating on the important genes that could be analyzed to help prevent or cure genetic diseases. Details of a rough map, they believed, could be filled in later.

Scientists at the HGP predicted that Venter's genome map would be full of holes. In addition, many felt that allowing patents on human genes was unethical, since no one should "own" the human genetic code. They also worried that his financial backers would file patents (exclusive rights to market inventions), limiting access to the information and thus blocking the advancement of science. Patents on genetic information could deter scientists from doing important research since only the company or government institution that holds a patent can profit from new discoveries that pertained to the patented information.

DNA strands. Medical scientists know of some 3,000 disorders that arise from errors in an individual's DNA. Much money and research went into studying human genes in the 1990s. Reproduced by permission of the Corbis Corporation.

The promise of these lucrative rights and scientific prestige drove researchers in the private and public sector to hasten their efforts toward a finished map of the human genome. Only after Venter met with Collins did the two sides agree that cooperation would achieve more than competition. So on June 26, 2000, Celera and HGP jointly announced the completion of a rough draft of the human genome, having put together a sequence of about 90 percent.

Total project completion—closing all of the remaining gaps and improving the map's accuracy—is expected in 2003. All researchers agree that once the gene sequence is completed, the next step will be to look into how genes vary from one person to the next, in effect, decoding the genetic basis of human individuality.

❖ THE INTERNET

The revolutionary technology of the Internet and the World Wide Web created a whole new digital culture in America during the 1990s. The idea of an "Information Superhighway" that could link anyone in the world through nearly instantaneous data transmission became a reality. Terms such as "cyberspace" and "the Net" became part of everyday speech. The introduction of the Internet into mainstream American society changed the ways in which business was conducted, information was exchanged, and social interactions were carried out.

Joseph C. R. Licklider, a psychologist at Massachusetts Institute of Technology (M.I.T.), first conceived the idea of an Internet, or an interconnected computer network, in 1962. He envisioned a globally interconnected set of computers through which anyone with a computer terminal could quickly access data and programs from another computer. That year, Licklider became the first head of the computer research program at the Advanced Research Projects Agency (ARPA), a bureau of the U.S. Department of Defense. Created in 1958 by President Dwight D. Eisenhower (1890–1969), ARPA was the first U.S. response to the Soviet launching of the unmanned satellite *Sputnik 1* in October 1957. This marked the beginning of the space race between the United States and the former Soviet Union.

The mission of ARPA was to ensure that the United States maintained a lead in applying state-of-the-art technology for military purposes and to prevent technological surprises from an enemy. In 1969, scientists at ARPA created the first-ever computer network, known as the ARPANET, which linked a total of four university and military computers. Within a year, twenty-three host computers were linked.

The major characteristic of ARPANET, and one of the key innovations that made the Internet possible, was the way it used the new idea called "packet switching." Data, or information to be transmitted from one computer to another, were divided into pieces or "packets" of equal-size message units, then launched into the network. Each packet was like a postcard carrying some part of the message. The packets found their way through the network along any paths that were open to them, moving from node to node along the network. A node was like a post office that sent the postcards along toward the recipient. Each node kept copies of the packets and continued to send them out until the packets successfully reached the next node. When all of the packets reached the final destination, they were reassembled and the complete message was delivered to the recipient. For defense purposes, this system seemed ideal since if there were any working path to the final destination, no matter how indirect, the new network would find it and use it to get the message through.

As this system slowly grew, it became apparent that eventually the computers at each different location would need to follow the same rules and procedures if they were to communicate with one another. In fact, if they all went their separate ways and spoke a different "language" and operated under different instructions, then they could never really be linked together in any meaningful way. More and more, the scientists, engineers, librarians, and computer experts who were then using ARPANET found that the network was both highly complex and very difficult to use. As early as 1972, users were beginning to form a sort of bulletin board for what we now call E-mail (electronic mail). This made the need for common procedures even more obvious, and in 1974, what came to be called a common protocol was finally developed. Protocols are sets of rules that standardize how something is done so that everyone knows what to do and what to expect. This common language was known as Transmission Control Protocol/Internet Protocol (TCP/IP).

The development of this protocol proved to be a crucial step in the development of a working network since it established certain rules or procedures that eventually would allow the network to expand. One of the keys of the protocol was that it was designed with what was called "open architecture." This meant that each small network could be separately designed and developed on its own and not have to modify itself in any way in order to be part of the overall network. This would be taken care of by a "gateway" (usually a larger computer) that each network would have whose special software linked it to the outside world. In order to make sure that data were transmitted quickly, the gateway software was designed so that it would not hold on to any of the data that passed through it. This not only sped things up, but it also removed any possibility of censorship or central control. There was no board of directors that dictated how the Internet could be used or what information could be passed along it. Finally, data would always follow the fastest available route, and all networks were allowed to participate. The Internet belonged to everyone.

The mid-1980s marked a boom in the personal computer industries. Inexpensive desktop machines and powerful network-ready servers allowed many companies to join the Internet for the first time. Corpora-

In 1995, Walt Disney Pictures released the huge hit film *Toy Story*, the first full-length animated feature to be created entirely by artists using computer tools and technology instead of drawing scenes by hand. The completely computer-generated movie took four years to make, lasted seventy-seven minutes, and contained 1,561 computer-generated images. To create the movie, Disney teamed up with Pixar Animation Studios, a pioneer in computer graphics and the first digital animation studio in the world. Using their own proprietary software, with computers as their tools, the moviemakers introduced a three-dimensional animation look, with qualities of texture, color, vibrant lighting, and details never before seen in traditional animated features.

tions began to use the Internet to communicate with each other and with their customers. Throughout the 1980s, more and more small networks were linked to the Internet, including those of the National Science Foundation, the National Aeronautics and Space Administration, the National Institutes of Health, and many foreign, educational, and commercial networks. The nodes in the growing Internet were divided up into Internet "domains," known as "mil," "org," "com," "gov," "edu," and "net." "Gov," "mil," and "edu" denoted government, military, and educational institutions, which were the pioneers of the Internet. "Com" stood for commercial institutions that were soon joining in, along with nonprofit organizations, or "orgs." "Net" computers served as gateways between networks.

In 1990, ARPANET was decommissioned, leaving the vast network of networks called the Internet. Although growing, the Internet at this time was no place for a beginner. The main problem was that every time users wanted to do something different on it (such as E-mail or file transfer), they had to know how to operate an entirely separate program. Commands had to be either memorized or reference manuals had to be consulted constantly. The Internet was not "user-friendly."

The development of what came to be called the World Wide Web in 1991 marked the real breakthrough of the Internet to a mass audience of users. The World Wide Web is a software package that was based on "hypertext." In hypertext, links are "embedded" in the text (meaning that

The development of what came to be called the World Wide Web in 1991 marked the real breakthrough of the Internet to a mass audience of users, including children.
Reproduced by permission of Archive Photos, Inc.

certain key words are either underlined or appear in a contrasting different color). The user can click on these links with a mouse to be taken to another site containing more information. The World Wide Web made the Internet simple to understand and enabled even new users to be able to explore or "surf" the Net.

MP3 Rocks the Music World

The Moving Picture Experts' Group, Audio Layer III (MP3), is a computer format that compresses tens of megabytes (MB) of an audio file into just a few megabytes. A standard MP3 compression is at a 10:1 ratio and yields a file that is about 4 MB for a three-minute audio track. MP3 technology started in the mid-1980s, but the format did not take off until the first MP3 player was developed in 1997. The following year, when a free MP3 music player software program was offered on the Internet, high-quality digital audio files became easily downloadable, and MP3 became the most popular trend in consumer audio. Soon the Internet was full of Web sites offering players and files. Chief among these was Napster, which offered Internet users just about any type of music they wanted for free.

Music industry executives quickly became concerned about MP3, arguing that it was being used to steal intellectual property. Many Web sites offered songs without first obtaining copyright permission, posing a major threat to record labels and performers. Record companies launched efforts in 1998 and 1999 to bring under control what they saw as bootlegging. Some recording artists, however, felt that MP3 might be a good thing, introducing a new way to bring their music to the public. Many musicians saw the MP3 technology as a way to sidestep the powerful music publishing business by using the Internet to distribute their songs. In 1998, record companies sued the makers of a portable MP3 player in an effort to keep the player off the market, but they lost the case. Undaunted, the music industry continued its fight against MP3-related businesses into the twenty-first century.

In 1993, the addition of the program called Mosaic proved to be the final breakthrough in terms of the Internet's ease-of-use. Before Mosaic, the Web was limited to only text or words. However, as a "graphical browser," the Mosaic program included multimedia links, meaning that a user could now view pictures, hear audio transmissions, and even see video transmissions. Before Mosaic, there were only fifty Web pages on the Internet. After its release, the World Wide Web grew by an astronomical 341,000 percent. By 1999, there were more than eleven million domain names registered on the Web and more than seventy million Web sites. In thirty years, the Internet grew from a military concept for communicating after a nuclear war to an Information Superhighway that ushered in a social and economic revolution.

❖ THE ENVIRONMENT: FROM GLOBAL WARMING TO THE EARTH SUMMIT

During the 1990s, global warming became a major concern for scientists and the public. Many scientists warned that carbon dioxide and other gases released from the burning of fossil fuels (coal, oil, and natural gas) were collecting in the atmosphere and acting like the glass walls of a greenhouse, trapping heat on the surface of Earth (a phenomenon known as the greenhouse effect). They predicted that average atmospheric temperatures could rise as much as 6.3 degrees Fahrenheit over the next century. If this occurred, the polar ice caps would melt, threatening coastal areas with flooding and causing massive climate changes throughout the world.

They cited evidence during the decade of increasing heat waves, melting polar ice, and rising sea levels—all thought to be caused by global warming. In Antarctica, Adelie penguin populations declined 33 percent over a twenty-five year period because the sea ice where they lived was shrinking. In Bermuda and Hawaii, rising seas killed coastal mangrove forests and caused beach erosion. In the late 1990s, scientists studying Arctic ice discovered that the polar ice was less than half as thick as ice measured in the same area in earlier years, down from between six and nine feet to less than four feet thick. They also found that the water below the ice contained far less salt than normal, indicating that the ice was melting at an alarming rate, flooding the sea with fresh water. Scientists had known for some time that the Arctic ice cap was shrinking, especially since 1990, but did not expect the changes to be as great as they appeared.

Skeptics questioned the presumed connection between human activity and global warming, arguing that while the global temperature might be rising, it could be the result of normal changes in weather patterns. They pointed out that Earth had undergone several major climate shifts throughout its known history and suggested that these normal shifts, not the burning of fossil fuels, were responsible for the changes in global-weather patterns.

Scientific experiments and research, as well as international conferences throughout the decade, addressed growing concerns about global warming. Although most climatologists (scientists who study changes in Earth's atmosphere) accepted the theory that the burning of fossil fuels and the subsequent rise in carbon dioxide levels in the atmosphere was causing the planet to grow warmer, there was no agreement on how global

The Birth of the DVD

DVD-Video (digital versatile disc or digital video disc) is a high-capacity multimedia data-storage medium designed to accommodate a complete movie on a single disc, as well as rich multimedia and high-quality audio. DVD technology originated in 1994 as two competing formats, Super Disc (SD) and Multimedia CD (MMCD). In 1995, developers agreed on a single format called DVD, and in 1997 it became publicly available in the United States, quickly becoming the most popular electronics consumer item to date.

DVD-Video (often simply called DVD), the first widely used application in the country, was embraced by the movie industry, which wanted a disc, like a compact disc (CD), capable of holding a high-quality recording of a full-length feature with surround-sound audio. The disc was played on a DVD player hooked up to a standard television set, much like the older videocassette recorder (VCR). By the end of the 1990s, DVD-ROM (read-only memory), the format for delivering data and multimedia content that could be played by computers equipped with DVD-ROM drives, was forecast to grow even faster than DVD-Video. With its capacity to hold the increasingly complex multimedia applications being developed, DVD-ROM was used widely in the computer industry and for new video games with better and more realistic video content. The DVD-Audio format, designed to provide the highest possible audio fidelity capable, far exceeding the quality of conventional CDs, was introduced in 1999.

warming might be reversed. America and the industrialized world had, since the nineteenth century, become too dependent on coal, oil, and natural gas to change its ways easily.

A totally enclosed greenhouse, Biosphere 2, was designed to mimic conditions on Earth (Biosphere 1) in a sealed, controlled environment. One of the most spectacular structures ever built, it is located in the Sonoran Desert at the foot of the Santa Catalina Mountains not far from Tucson, Arizona. It is the world's largest greenhouse, made of tubular steel and glass, covering an area of three football fields and rising to a height of eighty-five feet above the desert floor. Within the structure, there is a human habitat with a farm for the biospherians, or inhabitants, to work to provide their own food. There are also five other wild habitats or biomes representing a savannah, a rain forest, a marsh, a desert, and an ocean. Biosphere 2 is completely sealed so no air or moisture can flow in or out. Nearby are two balloon-like structures that operate like a pair of lungs for Biosphere 2 by maintaining air pressure inside. Only sunlight and electricity are provided from outside.

On September 26, 1991, four women and four men from three different countries entered the Biosphere 2 and the doors were sealed for the two-year-long initial program of survival and experimentation. During this time, the biospherians attempted to run the farm and grow their own food in the company of some pigs and goats and many chickens. They shared the other biomes with over four thousand species of animals and plants that were native to those habitats. The resident scientists observed the interactions of plants and animals, their reactions to change, and their unique methods of living. The biospherians also had the assignment of experimenting with new methods of cleaning air and water.

On September 26, 1993, the biospherians emerged from Biosphere 2. It had been the longest period on record that humans had lived in an "isolated confined environment." Unfortunately, the experiment did not live up to expectations. Oxygen levels inside the complex dropped so low that supplemental oxygen had to be added to protect the lives of the eight biospherians—violating the idea of total isolation. An unusually cloudy year in the Arizona desert stunted food production in Biosphere 2, because the plants needed sunlight, and some reports suggested that scientists smuggled in extra food. Nearly all of the birds, animals, and insects that were brought into the environment and expected to thrive there died instead, though ants and cockroaches ran rampant. In 1996, Columbia University took over operation of the facility, using it as a teaching and research tool for environmental science education and research.

In 1992, representatives from more than 172 nations met in Rio de Janeiro, Brazil, for the first United Nations Conference on Environment and Development (UNCED), or International Earth Summit. This meeting was held to address problems of environmental protection and how worldwide economic development can be achieved without sacrificing the environment. The assembled leaders discussed global issues ranging from an increase in population to global warming to protecting the world's plant and animal species. The Earth Summit met with mixed success. Critics charged that the most advanced countries, including the United States, were trying to regulate the development of poorer countries without improving their own environmental performance.

In 1997, the United Nations issued a five-year review of the progress of Earth Summit agreements. One of the findings of the review indicated

OPPOSITE PAGE
Biosphere 2 in Tucson, Arizona. **Reproduced by permission of the Metropolitan Tucson Convention and Visitors Bureau.**

that global water supplies could be in danger. The supply of fresh, clean water, already threatened by growing levels of pollution, was found to be growing so scarce in some areas that two-thirds of humanity could suffer moderate to severe water shortages by 2030.

❖ A WIRELESS WORLD

Mobile, or wireless, communications became a significant part of American life during the 1990s. At the end of the decade, a poll showed that the mobile or cellular phone was the most important new personal communications device for many Americans. Most respondents cited cell phones as the technology that they used most in their daily lives, more than a computer, E-mail, or the Internet. Cellular telephones became ever smaller and more portable, and could be carried inconspicuously. Lower costs and greater convenience gained millions of new customers for mobile-phone technology every year. By 1995, there were approximately eighty-five million users of cellular telephony worldwide, and thirty-two million of them were Americans. As of June 1999, there were more than seventy-six million wireless communications subscribers in the United States, with 38 percent of these using digital wireless technology.

The term cellular comes from the design of the system that carries mobile phone calls from geographical service areas that are divided into smaller pockets, called cells. Each cell contains a base station that accepts and transfers the calls from mobile phones that are based in its cell. The cells are interconnected by a central controller, which is called the mobile telecommunications switching office (MTSO). The MTSO connects the cellular system to the conventional telephone network, and it also records call information so that the system's users can be charged appropriate fees. In addition, the MTSO enables the signal strength to be examined every few seconds (automatically by computer) and then be switched to a stronger cell if necessary. The user does not notice the "handoff" from one cell to another.

Traditional cellular technology uses analog service. This type of service transmits calls in one continuous stream of information between the mobile phone and the base station on the same frequency. Analog technology modulates (varies) radio signals so that they can carry information such as the human voice. The major drawback to using analog service is the limitation on the number of channels that can be used.

Digital technology, on the other hand, uses a simple binary code to represent any signal as a sequence of ones and zeros. The smallest unit of information for the digital transmission system is called a bit, which is either one or zero. Digital technology encodes the user's voice into a bit stream. By breaking down the information into these small units, digital technology allows data to be transmitted faster and in a more secure form than analog.

Scientists at Bell Laboratories had invented cellular technology in the late 1940s, but the growth of wireless communications did not begin until

One of the biggest concerns during the last year of the 1990s was the Y2K bug (Y2K was the nickname for the year 2000: Y for year and 2 times K, the standard symbol for one thousand). The so-called Y2K bug was a fault built into computer software because early developers of computer programs were uncertain that computers would even have a future. To save on memory and storage, these developers abbreviated standardized dates with two digits each for the day, month, and year. For instance, October 14, 1966, was read as 101466. However, this short form could also mean October 14, 1066, or October 14, 2066.

As early as 1997, it had been officially determined that many computers, from those operating in agencies of the federal government to those found in individual homes, might not recognize the year 2000. Experts feared widespread simultaneous crashing of systems everywhere from Automatic Teller Machines (ATMs) to electrical grids and hospital equipment to the possible accidental detonation of atomic weapons. To ease the public's concerns, businesses and government agencies issued "Y2K ready" statements, meaning their computer had been reprogrammed to handle the date change.

For some people, though, the Y2K problem signaled nothing less than the possible end of the world. All over the country, people stocked up on power generators, dried and canned food, bottled water, guns, and ammunition in preparation for a possible New Year's Day that would begin in chaos. Y2K fears spawned a host of associated products and businesses from survival videos to advisory Web sites to agencies that, for a fee, reserved places in Y2K-safe communities. Most Americans, however, took the whole thing in stride. As early as January 1999, almost 40 percent of people surveyed believed that the Y2K problem was not something about which to be terribly concerned. In the end, it wasn't.

1983, when the Federal Communications Commission (FCC, government department in charge of regulating anything that goes out over the airwaves, such as telephone, television, and radio) authorized commercial cellular service in the United States. Bell Laboratory's Advance Mobile Phone System (AMPS), the first commercial analog cellular service, became a reality, and mobile phones began to be used throughout North America, mainly by business executives in their automobiles. During the 1980s and early 1990s, regions of the world such as Western Europe and Latin America also began to develop wireless communications. By the end of the decade, mobile phone use was widespread among the general population.

With the rise of cellular use, however, American society was confronted with a host of new problems resulting from noisy phones and beepers going off everywhere from churches to classrooms to movie theaters to restaurants. Perhaps the biggest problem debated was the use of cellular phones while driving. According to a study published in the *New England Journal of Medicine,* people talking on a cellular phone while driving were four times more likely to be in an accident than the average driver. Those odds placed the cellular-phone driver on the same level as a drunk driver. Several state legislatures and city halls proposed bills that would ban the use of cellular phones while driving.

❖ NASA: PROBE FAILURES, HUBBLE, AND THE ISS

Facing criticisms early in the decade that it was wasting money, the National Aeronautics and Space Administration (NASA) announced that it would find ways to do more with less. The administration's mantra became "faster, better, cheaper." Indeed, NASA had great successes during the decade, including the space probe *Mars Pathfinder,* built for a tenth of the cost of its predecessors and hailed as a huge success. The probe landed on the surface of Mars on July 4, 1997, and released the Sojourner rover, the first independent vehicle to travel on another planet. The probe and rover sent back to Earth sixteen thousand images and 2.6 billion bits of information about the Martian terrain, including chemical analyses of rocks and the soil. In addition, John Glenn, U.S. senator and the first American to orbit Earth, returned to space in 1998 aboard the NASA space shuttle *Discovery* to a surge of public approval.

The space agency, however, did suffer some humiliating losses during the decade. The $194 million *Mars Polar Lander,* with the Deep Space 2 Probe, was launched on January 3, 1999 and lost on December 3 because of a software glitch in the probe's computer. Worse, perhaps, was the catastrophic failure of the *Mars Climate Orbiter,* launched December 11, 1998, and lost in September 1999. The primary cause of the failure was that the builder of the spacecraft, Lockheed Martin, provided one set of specifications in old-fashioned English units, while its operators at the NASA Jet Propulsion Laboratory were using the metric system. The report on the failure also uncovered management problems that let the mistake go undiscovered, including poor communication between mission teams, insufficient training, and inadequate staffing. With the "faster, better,

OPPOSITE PAGE
The Hubble Space Telescope with Earth in the background.
Reproduced by permission of Archive Photos, Inc.

cheaper" approach, the navigation team was seriously overworked trying to run three missions at once.

One significant NASA project in the 1990s was the Hubble Space Telescope (HST), which began as a failure but ended as a success. Astronauts aboard the space shuttle *Discovery* in 1990 released the Hubble Space Telescope into orbit 370 miles above Earth. Because it did not have to look through the distorting prism of the atmosphere, the HST could view objects with greater brightness, clarity, and detail than any telescope on Earth. The mission initially appeared to be a failure, as scientists learned shortly after the HST began orbiting Earth that the curve in its primary mirror was off by just a fraction of a hair's width. This flaw caused light to reflect away from the center of the mirror. As a result, the HST produced blurry pictures.

In 1993, astronauts aboard the space shuttle *Endeavor* caught up with the HST and installed three coin-sized mirrors around the primary mirror, which brought the light into proper focus. In 1997, another space shuttle crew conducted general repairs to the HST. Then in November 1999, the HST stopped working after its gyroscopes broke down. Without the gyroscopes, the telescope could not hold steady while focusing on stars, galaxies, and other cosmic targets. A month later, during an eight-day mission, astronauts aboard the space shuttle *Discovery* installed almost $70 million worth of new equipment on the HST.

Despite the need for repairs, the HST has proven to be the finest of all telescopes ever produced. The thousands of images it has captured—a comet hitting Jupiter, a nursery where stars are born, stars that belong to no galaxy, galaxies that house quasars, galaxies violently colliding—have amazed astronomers. It allowed scientists to look deeper into space than ever before, providing evidence that supported the big bang theory (the idea that the universe was created in a violent event approximately twelve to fifteen billion years ago), and indicating that the universe could be younger than previously thought. It also identified disks of dust around young stars that suggested an abundance of planets in the universe, which might mean a greater chance of life in outer space.

The beginning of the International Space Station (ISS) project was another great achievement for NASA during the 1990s. A cooperative project involving the United States, Russia, Canada, Japan, and twelve other countries, the ISS was billed as a "city in space." First conceived by NASA in 1983, the project went through many design changes and consumed large sums of money before the first piece was ever built. As envisioned in the 1990s, the station would eventually extend more three times the length of a football field and weigh more than one million pounds when

American Nobel Prize Winners in Chemistry or Physics

Year	Scientist(s)	Field
1990	Elias James Corey	Chemistry
	Jerome I. Friedman	Physics
	Henry W. Kendall	
1991	No awards given to an American	
1992	Rudolph A. Marcus	Chemistry
1993	Kary B. Mullis	Chemistry
	Russell A. Hulse	Physics
	Joseph H. Taylor Jr.	
1994	George A. Olah	Chemistry
	Clifford G. Shull	Physics
1995	Mario J. Molina	Chemistry
	F. Sherwood Rowland	
	Martin L. Perl	Physics
	Frederick Reines	
1996	Robert F. Curl	Chemistry
	Richard E. Smalley	
	David M. Lee	Physics
	Douglas D. Osheroff	
	Robert C. Richardson	
1997	Paul D. Boyer	Chemistry
	Steven Chu	Physics
	William D. Phillips	
1998	Walter Kohn	Chemistry
	Robert B. Laughlin	Physics
	Daniel C. Tsui	
1999	Ahmed H. Zewail	Chemistry

completed. It would serve as a permanent Earth-orbiting laboratory that will allow humans to perform long-term scientific research in outer space.

On November 20, 1998, a Russian Proton rocket blasted off from the Baikonur Cosmodrome in Kazakhstan, carrying the first piece of the station: the Zarya (Sunrise) module, designed to provide the initial power, communications, and propulsion for the station. The second piece, the Unity connecting module, was brought into orbit a month later by a U.S.

shuttle. By the end of the decade, the joint program was awaiting the launch of the Russian service module that would house hundreds of astronauts and cosmonauts over the life of the station. The key source of energy for the station was to be solar panels.

Critics charged that the station was too expensive, with an overall initial cost of $40 to $60 billion, and an estimated $98-billion cost for the fifteen-year life of the project (scheduled to be completed in 2006). Other detractors said the station had little real utility. It would be too expensive to manufacture anything aboard, and scientific experiments could be done more cheaply if the station were automated. Supporters of the project argued that it would allow for unprecedented scientific experiments in the near-zero gravity of space and serve as a platform for space-based innovations in the twenty-first century.

 For More Information

BOOKS

Alling, Abigail, and Mark Nelson with Sally Silverstone. *Life Under Glass: The Inside Story of Biosphere 2.* Oracle, AZ: Biosphere Press, 1993.

Cherfas, Jeremy. *Essential Science: The Human Genome.* New York: DK Publishing, 2002.

Harland, David M., and John E. Catchpole. *Creating the International Space Station.* New York: Springer Verlag, 2002.

McCormick, Anita Louise. *The Internet: Surfing the Issues.* Berkeley Heights, NJ: Enslow Publishers, 1998.

Pringle, Laurence P. *Global Warming: The Threat of Earth's Changing Climate.* SeaStar Books, 2001.

WEB SITES

Columbia University Biosphere 2 Center. http://www.bio2.edu/ (accessed on May 25, 2002).

Earth Summit. http://www.un.org/geninfo/bp/enviro.html (accessed on May 25, 2002).

EPA Global Warming Site. http://www.epa.gov/globalwarming/ (accessed on May 25, 2002).

HSF-International Space Station. http://spaceflight.nasa.gov/station/ (accessed on May 25, 2002).

Hubble Space Telescope Project. http://hubble.nasa.gov/ (accessed on May 25, 2002).

Human Genome Project Information. http://www.ornl.gov/hgmis/ (accessed on May 25, 2002).

Nobel e-Museum http://www.nobel.se/index.html (accessed on May 25, 2002).

chapter eight *Sports*

1990: January 15 Joe Montana sets the NFL record for postseason touchdowns with numbers thirty and thirty-one, breaking Terry Bradshaw's record.

1990: June 11 Nolan Ryan of the Texas Rangers pitches his sixth no-hit game, a major league baseball record, against the Oakland Athletics.

1990: October 28 Fourteen-year-old Jennifer Capriati wins her first professional tennis tournament, the Puerto Rican Open.

1991: March 2 Del Ballard Jr. throws the most famous gutter ball in Professional Bowlers Association history in the finals of the Fair Lanes Open. Needing only seven pins to win, Ballard hits the gutter instead, losing the thirty-thousand-dollar first prize.

1991: July 15 Sandhi Ortiz-DelValle becomes the first woman to officiate a men's professional basketball game.

1992: February 8 to 23 The Winter Olympics are held in Albertville, France.

1992: July 25 to August 9 The Summer Olympics are held in Barcelona, Spain.

1992: November 29 Jerry Rice, wide receiver for the San Francisco 49ers, catch-es his one-hundredth touchdown pass.

1993: April 30 Monica Seles, while playing in a tennis match in Hamburg, Germany, is stabbed by a rival's fan.

1993: September 22 The expansion Colorado Rockies franchise sets a major league baseball attendance record of 4,483,350 during the team's first season.

1993: November 14 Don Shula breaks George Halas's career victory mark as an NFL coach with win number 325.

1994: February 12 to 27 The Winter Olympics are held in Lillehammer, Norway.

1994: August 12 Major league baseball players go on strike to protest the owners' plan for a salary cap. The season is ended and the World Series is canceled for the first time in ninety years.

1994: October 31 Because she was winning every junior tennis tournament she entered, Venus Williams turns professional at age fourteen.

1995: March 19 Michael Jordan, who had retired the previous year to play baseball for the Chicago White Sox, returns to professional basketball to play for the Chicago Bulls.

1995: August 20 Joe Mesa, pitching for the Cleveland Indians, gets his thirty-seventh save in thirty-seven opportunities and sets a new major league baseball record.

1995: September 6 Cal Ripken Jr., an infielder for the Baltimore Orioles, plays in his 2,131st consecutive major league baseball game, breaking Lou Gehrig's record.

1996: July 19 to August 4 The Summer Olympics are held in Atlanta, Georgia.

1996: September 18 Roger Clemens, pitcher for the Boston Red Sox, ties his own major league record of twenty strikeouts in a nine-inning game.

1996: November 23 Coach Pat Summitt wins her six-hundredth women's college basketball game while coaching the University of Tennessee Lady Volunteers.

1997: April 9 Tiger Woods wins the Masters golf tournament with a record eighteen-under-par.

1997: June 28 Evander Holyfield wins a heavyweight fight against Mike Tyson when Tyson is disqualified for biting Holyfield's ear.

1997: October 28 Dee Kantner and Violet Palmer make history by becoming the first female referees in the NBA.

1998: February 7 to 22 The Winter Olympics are held in Nagano, Japan.

1998: March 1 Venus Williams wins her first professional tennis singles title in the IGA Tennis Classic.

1998: September 8 Mark McGwire of the St. Louis Cardinals breaks Roger Maris's single-season home run record, hitting number sixty-two.

1999: July 10 Brandi Chastain's penalty kick leads the U.S. soccer team to victory over China in the Women's World Cup.

1999: July 25 Cyclist Lance Armstrong makes an amazing comeback after battling testicular cancer to win the Tour de France, the world's premier cycling event.

1999: December 26 Michael Jordan is selected by the Entertainment and Sports Programming Network (ESPN) as the greatest North American athlete of the twentieth century.

Overview

Most of what was newsworthy in 1990s sports had little to do with the field of play. Professional athletics had become big business, and the business of athletics kept getting bigger. Big cities paid for huge stadiums to lure league franchises. Even smaller cities built new minor-league ballparks to promote the economic boom associated with sports. Team owners and players made huge amounts of money, only to demand even more. A strike in baseball over player salaries resulted in the cancellation of the World Series for the first time in ninety years. Competition in sports seemed to be defined by the bottom line, not the box score. Not surprisingly, the most successful sports movie of the decade, *Jerry Maguire* (1996), was not about an athlete but a fictional sports agent. His client's motto spoke for the decade: "Show me the money."

On a different front, scandals in sports sunk to unprecedented depths of sordidness. Tonya Harding was implicated in an attack on her figure-skating competitor Nancy Kerrigan. Kerrigan's attacker intended, but failed, to keep her out of Olympic competition. Even the Olympics, once a model of virtue, suffered a black eye when evidence came to light that International Olympic Committee officials had accepted bribes from cities seeking to host the Games. Boxer Mike Tyson behaved badly in and out of the ring; after he was convicted of rape and sent to prison, he partially bit off his opponent's ear during a bout. Basketball player Latrell Sprewell attacked and choked his coach, P. J. Carlesimo. Drug abuse among athletes, especially of muscle-building steroids, and rampant criminal behavior plagued sports at every level.

All of the attention on big money and poor behavior did not mean that baseball, basketball, football, golf, and hockey shut down for the decade. Baseball had some of its greatest moments ever because of Cal Ripken Jr., Mark McGwire, and Sammy Sosa. Michael Jordan, arguably the greatest player in the history of basketball (who also was voted by ESPN as the Athlete of the Century), was on the court for much of the decade and on the baseball diamond for one fascinating, if undistinguished, year. Football thrived at every level, and continued to be the nation's most popular sport. Golf, in need of rejuvenation, welcomed Tiger Woods into its professional ranks after he had decimated his amateur competitors for three years running. Ice hockey expanded into the southern and western states, becoming a truly national sport for the first time. Tennis, a thoroughly international sport, saw many Americans winning Grand Slam titles throughout the decade, and American Pete Sampras dominated the men's game. The Summer and Winter Olympic Games were separated by a two-year span for the first time in 1994, rather than taking place in the same calendar year as they had in the past. The United States hosted the Summer Games during the decade in Atlanta, Georgia, in 1996. Carl Lewis, Bonnie Blair, Kristi Yamaguchi, Dan Jansen, Shannon Miller, Michael Johnson, Picabo Street, and others won Olympic gold medals for the United States during the 1990s.

Sports for women, featuring some spectacularly capable athletes, emerged into the national consciousness during the decade. Athletes such as Mia Hamm (soccer), Lindsay Davenport (tennis), Picabo Street (skiing), Brandi Chastain (soccer), Sheryl Swoopes (basketball), Bonnie Blair (speed skating), Betsy King (golf), Tara Lipinski (figure skating), Venus and Serena Williams (tennis), and Jackie Joyner-Kersee (track and field) became household names. Attendance at women's sporting events also shot up. On July 10, 1999, the Women's World Cup soccer championship competition, in which the U.S. team defeated China, was played before 90,185 fans at the Rose Bowl in Pasadena, California.

Lance Armstrong (1971–) Lance Armstrong was the highest-ranked cyclist in the world in 1996 when he was diagnosed with testicular cancer, which quickly spread to his lungs and brain. Given a fifty-fifty chance of survival, he underwent surgeries as well as aggressive chemotherapy treatment to remove the cancerous lesions. Five months later, Armstrong returned to cycling. In what many consider the greatest comeback in sports history, he won the prestigious Tour de France in July 1999. Only one other American, Greg LeMond, had ever won the grueling twenty-stage road race that covers more than two thousand miles over three weeks. *Photo reproduced by permission of AP/Wide World Photos.*

Jeff Gordon (1971–) Race car driver Jeff Gordon was the indisputable king of NASCAR during the last half of the 1990s. He had won Rookie of the Year honors on the Winston Cup circuit in 1993. The following year, he won his first NASCAR race, the Coca-Cola 600. He continued to finish first throughout the remainder of the decade. He became the youngest driver to win the Daytona 500 and was the first ever to win three consecutive Southern 500s, winning his fourth straight in 1998. At the end of the decade, NASCAR selected Gordon as "Driver of the '90s." *Photo reproduced by permission of AP/Wide World Photos.*

Mia Hamm (1972–) Mia Hamm dominated women's soccer from the end of the 1980s. While attending the University of North Carolina, she led the women's team to four straight NCAA championships (1989–93). After turning professional, she was honored as U.S. Soccer's Female Athlete of the Year each year from 1994 to 1998. After the U.S. women's soccer team won an Olympic gold medal in 1996, Hamm became a media celebrity, her face and form instantly recognizable across the country. In 1999, she and her U.S. teammates defeated China to win the World Cup, the worldwide soccer championship. *Photo reproduced by permission of Allsport Photography USA.*

Michael Jordan (1963–) Michael Jordan dominated professional basketball in the 1990s like no other athlete in any other sport. In the early part of the decade, he won two most valuable player (MVP) awards (1991, 1992), an Olympic gold medal (1992), and three NBA championships with the Chicago Bulls (1991–93). In 1993, at the peak of his career, he retired from basketball to pursue a career in professional baseball on the minor-league level. He returned to dominating basketball once again in 1995, helping lead the Bulls to three consecutive NBA titles (1996–98) and capturing MVP honors in 1996 and 1998. *Photo reproduced by permission of the Corbis Corporation.*

Greg Maddux (1966–) Pitcher Greg Maddux was the premier professional baseball player of the decade. He won the Cy Young award each year between 1992 and 1995, making him the only pitcher in the history of the game to win the prize four times in a row. He won four ERA (earned-run average) titles (1993–95, 1998) and recorded twelve consecutive seasons with at least fifteen wins and two hundred or more innings pitched. In 1994 and 1995, he became the first major league pitcher in seventy-six years to have an ERA of less than 1.80 in two consecutive seasons. *Photo reproduced by permission of AP/Wide World Photos.*

Pat Summitt (1952–) Pat Summitt, women's basketball coach at the University of Tennessee, is considered the best college basketball coach, male or female, in history. She coached her team to six NCAA championships, four during the 1990s (1991, 1996–98). The three consecutive titles were a first for any women's basketball program. On March 2, 1998, she appeared on the cover of *Sports Illustrated,* the first female coach to do so. As she concluded, her twenty-fifth season at Tennessee in 1999, she had amassed more than seven hundred victories, less than thirty shy of the all-time mark for a woman's coach. *Photo reproduced by permission of AP/Wide World Photos.*

Venus Williams (1980–) and Serena Williams (1981–) Sisters Venus Williams and Serena Williams began to rule the world of women's professional tennis in the late 1990s. Venus won her first singles title, the IGA Tennis Classic in 1998. By the end of the decade, she had won nine singles titles and more than two million dollars in prize money. Serena won a Grand Slam title, the U.S. Open (1999), before her older sister won one. In addition to their individual victories, Venus and Serena teamed up to win two Grand Slam doubles titles: the French Open (1999) and the U.S. Open (1999). *Photo of Venus Williams reproduced by permission of AP/Wide World Photos.*

Tiger Woods (1975–) Tiger Woods, who had turned professional in August 1996, won twenty-four professional golfing tournaments, fifteen of them on the PGA tour, by the end of the decade. He was the first player since 1990 to win two tour events in his first year as a pro and the first player since 1982 to record five straight top-five finishes. In 1997, he won the famed Masters tournament, the first African American and the youngest golfer to do so. In 1999, he became the first golfer since Ben Hogan in 1953 to win four consecutive PGA events. *Photo reproduced by permission of AP/Wide World Photos.*

◆ *Topics in the News*

❖ BASEBALL: STRIKES AND RECORD-BREAKERS

Baseball, the national pastime, went from the depths of despair to the heights of joy in the 1990s. Greed and money nearly caused the downfall of the sport. Strikes and work stoppages were nothing new to professional sports, and baseball had experienced its share of both in the previous decades. Beginning in August 1994, a 232-day strike by players wiped out the final 52 days and 669 games of the 1994 season and forced the cancellation of that year's World Series. It was only the second time in the history of major league baseball that the World Series was canceled (the first was in 1904) and the first time it was canceled due to a labor dispute. The strike also wiped out the first 252 games of the 1995 season, raising the total number of games lost to 921: the longest and costliest work stoppage in the history of professional sports.

The quarrel between owners and players arose from the owners' desire to impose a salary cap, which is an agreement that places an upper limit and sometimes a lower limit on the money each team can spend on player salaries. The owners' proposal was to limit each team's salaries to 50 percent of average team revenues. Before the strike, the players received 58 percent of average team revenues.

When baseball finally resumed on April 26, 1995, it did so amidst fan anger directed at players, owners, and baseball in general. Many fans stayed away from the ballparks that season, with attendance 20 percent lower than the previous year. Although average attendance did bounce back by the end of the decade, it never returned to its pre-strike levels.

Of course, moments of pure athletic achievement still delighted those baseball fans who stubbornly refused to boycott the game. Six different teams claimed the nine World Series titles awarded during the decade. The New York Yankees won three championships (1996, 1998, and 1999); in 1998 they won more games (114) than any other team in baseball history. The Atlanta Braves also had a good decade, getting to the World Series five times, but winning only once (1995). The most unexpected championship season was provided by the Florida Marlins, the first and only team in major league history to win the World Series (1997) after making the playoffs as a wild card.

Baseball in the 1990s was rescued by two unlikely events: the shattering of both the consecutive-games-played record and the single-season home-run record, marks that had stood for fifty-six and thirty-seven years, respectively. On September 6, 1995, at Camden Yards in Baltimore, Mary-

Year	Winning Team (League) Games Won	Losing Team (League) Games Won
1990	Cincinnati Reds (NL) 4	Oakland Athletics (AL) 0
1991	Minnesota Twins (AL) 4	Atlanta Braves (NL) 3
1992	Toronto Blue Jays (AL) 4	Atlanta Braves (NL) 2
1993	Toronto Blue Jays (AL) 4	Philadelphia Phillies (NL) 2
1994	No World Series held	
1995	Atlanta Braves (NL) 4	Clevelenad Indians (AL) 2
1996	New York Yankees (AL) 4	Atlanta Braves (NL) 2
1997	Florida Marlins (NL) 4	Cleveland Indians (AL) 3
1998	New York Yankees (AL) 4	San Diego Padres (NL) 0
1999	New York Yankees (AL) 4	Atlanta Braves (NL) 0

land, Cal Ripken Jr., one of baseball's most respected veterans, broke Lou Gehrig's cherished long-held record for consecutive games played. Gehrig, who had played for the New York Yankees, had set the record of 2,130 consecutive games played between 1925 and 1939. After Ripken had played four-and-one-half innings of the game (which made the game official in the record book), play was halted for thirty minutes as he trotted around the field, shaking hands and accepting applause from the delirious fans in the stands. To top it off, he then hit a home run in the sixth inning. Ripken eventually played in 2,632 straight games, ending the streak only when he benched himself on September 19, 1998.

The same year that Ripken's streak ended, Mark McGwire of the St. Louis Cardinals and Sammy Sosa of the Chicago Cubs chased each other to break another record: Roger Maris's sixty-one home runs during the 1961 season. During the summer of 1998, McGwuire and Sosa lit up the scoreboards of the National League, each hitting more home runs in a single season than any other person in history. During the chase for the record, 70,589,505 fans attended games, many of them filling ballparks specifically to cheer on McGwire and Sosa. People even came early to watch the two players, especially McGwire, in batting practice. McGwire did not just hit balls over the outfield fence—he knocked them out of the ballpark.

Mark McGwire, of the St. Louis Cardinals, hit more homeruns in a single season than any other person in history.
Reproduced by permission of Archive Photos, Inc.

The home-run race heated up when McGwire set the new mark of sixty-two on September 8 with his shortest home run of the season. On September 25 Sosa became the first major league player to hit sixty-six homers in one season, but he held that distinction for only forty-five minutes. Incredibly, McGwire hit five home runs in his last nineteen swings, finishing the season with an amazing seventy home runs. Throughout the

Top Twenty American Athletes of the Twentieth Century (as selected by ESPN)

1) Michael Jordan
2) Babe Ruth
3) Muhammad Ali
4) Jim Brown
5) Wayne Gretzky
6) Jesse Owens
7) Jim Thorpe
8) Willie Mays
9) Jack Nicklaus
10) Babe Didrikson
11) Joe Louis
12) Carl Lewis
13) Wilt Chamberlain
14) Hank Aaron
15) Jackie Robinson
16) Ted Williams
17) Magic Johnson
18) Bill Russell
19) Martina Navratilova
20) Ty Cobb

season both men displayed pure class. On the day that McGwire hit the home run that broke the record, Sosa ran in from the outfield (the fates had the two men playing on the same field that magical day) to bear-hug the man who had been his rival.

❖ BASKETBALL: I WANT TO BE LIKE MIKE

One man defined basketball in the 1990s: Michael Jordan. He was quite possibly the best athlete in the history of basketball. Opponents occasionally could block his shots, or outscore him in a given game, but Jordan ruled the sport throughout the decade. Everyone understood that the game would not be the same when Jordan retired, first in 1993, then again in 1999 after having returned to the game in 1995. The Chicago Bulls, largely because of Jordan, were the dominant team of the decade, leading the league in championships and even in merchandise sales. Other

1990s NBA Champions

Year	Winning Team/Games Won	Losing Team/Games Won
1990	Detroit Pistons 4	Portland Trail Blazers 1
1991	Chicago Bulls 4	Los Angeles Lakers 1
1992	Chicago Bulls 4	Portland Trail Blazers 2
1993	Chicago Bulls 4	Phoenix Suns 2
1994	Houston Rockets 4	New York Knicks 3
1995	Houston Rockets 4	Orlando Magic 0
1996	Chicago Bulls 4	Seattle SuperSonics 2
1997	Chicago Bulls 4	Utah Jazz 2
1998	Chicago Bulls 4	Utah Jazz 2
1999	San Antonio Spurs 4	New York Knicks 1

great players were a part of the mix at various times, including Horace Grant, Scottie Pippen, and Dennis Rodman. They also had an impressive coach in Phil Jackson. How these talented men might have succeeded without Jordan will never be known. For example, Jackson won six titles as Jordan's coach and none without him during the decade.

Jordan was not, however, the only story in the National Basketball Association (NBA). Magic Johnson and Larry Bird, who had saved basketball in the 1980s, ended their illustrious careers early in the decade. Charles Barkley, John Stockton, Shaquille O'Neal, David Robinson, Hakeem Olajuwon, Clyde Drexler, and Karl Malone all played magnificently. These players helped form the nucleus of two "Dream Teams," which represented the United States during the 1992 and 1996 Olympics, and they crushed their opponents to win two gold medals. The league seemed to become more competitive during Jordan's absence, as these and other players had the opportunity to face off.

Even with such talented players, however, professional basketball was usually a delight to behold when Jordan was on the court. In addition to the grace with which he played the game, he had the charisma to keep the public fascinated and tuned in. Yet none of the championship series in which the Bulls participated were blowouts. They always seemed vulnerable, which made Jordan's heroics that much more amazing. In the 1996 finals

1990s Super Bowl Champions

Year	Winning Team/Score	Losing Team/Score
1990	San Francisco 49ers 55	Denver Broncos 10
1991	New York Giants 20	Buffalo Bills 19
1992	Washington Redskins 37	Buffalo Bills 24
1993	Dallas Cowboys 52	Buffalo Bills 17
1994	Dallas Cowboys 30	Buffalo Bills 13
1995	San Francisco 49ers 49	San Diego Chargers 26
1996	Dallas Cowboys 27	Pittsburgh Steelers 17
1997	Green Bay Packers 35	New England Patriots 21
1998	Denver Broncos 31	Green Bay Packers 24
1999	Denver Broncos 34	Atlanta Falcons 19

against the Utah Jazz, Jordan faced Malone, who had won the most valuable player (MVP) award that season. In the series, Jordan averaged thirty-two points per game, hitting the buzzer-beater in the first game, scoring thirty-eight points in the fifth game despite being ill, scoring another thirty-nine points in the sixth and final game, and earning MVP honors for the series.

It took all of Jordan's magic to overcome the bad feelings of fans toward professional basketball resulting from other incidents. Latrell Sprewell's choking assault on his Golden State Warriors coach P. J. Carlesimo on December 1, 1997, and his threats to kill Carlesimo, came across to the fans as typical behavior of spoiled, rich athletes with whom spectators had little in common. It was impossible for many fans to believe that NBA stars were average men who had managed to succeed with hard work and talent. Clearly, such athletes were far from average. When a dispute between management and players threatened to halt play in 1999, it became hard for fans to imagine paying hundreds of dollars to attend a game while billionaire owners and millionaire athletes demanded a greater share of the profits.

❖ FOOTBALL: IN WITH THE NEW

The 1990s was a decade of expansion and change for the National Football League (NFL). New franchises and stadiums, additional wild-

Barry Sanders, running back for the Detroit Lions, rushed for over one thousand yards in ten consecutive seasons (1989–1998), setting an NFL record. Reproduced by permission of AP/Wide World Photos.

card teams in the playoffs, expanding television coverage, and increased audiences and attendance all meant more money for the owners and players. It also meant higher ticket prices for the fans. Several teams moved from their home markets to new cities (for example, the Rams from Los Angeles to St. Louis) in search of better facilities, higher attendance, and other financial reasons. The Jacksonville Jaguars and the Carolina Panthers joined the league, and Cleveland was awarded a new team (although they kept their old name, the Browns) after the former Cleveland franchise had moved to Baltimore (to become the Ravens). With all the expansion and moving, some thought the league had been watered-down. Others thought it had been made more exciting.

Off-the-field criminal activities, ranging from drug offenses to domestic abuse, damaged the reputations of many players during the decade. The league fined players for shoving referees during games and for taking part in senseless fistfights away from the stadiums. In July 1999, three members of the New York Jets were arrested following a bar fight. Current and former players were cited for possession of drugs, driving while intoxicated, and violent actions. Several players even attacked and wounded fellow teammates in practice sessions. Most seriously, Rae Carruth, a wide receiver for the Carolina Panthers, went on trial for the drive-by shooting murder of his girlfriend, who was pregnant with their child, on November 16, 1999. He was eventually convicted and sentenced in January 2001 to serve at least twenty years in prison.

In spite of these players' horrendous activities, NFL football continued to be the most popular spectator sport in the country. The decade began with perennial powers the San Francisco 49ers, the New York Giants, the Washington Redskins, and the Dallas Cowboys winning Super Bowls. Dallas won three (1993, 1994, and 1996) and San Francisco two (1990 and 1995). The Giants (1991) and Redskins (1992) each won one, as did the Green Bay Packers (1997), the team's first title in twenty-nine years. The Packers' victory was widely hailed as a deserved reward for faithful Packer fans and quarterback Brett Favre, a three-time league MVP. When the American Football Conference (AFC) Denver Broncos, led by quarterback John Elway, won the Super Bowl in 1998, they broke the stranglehold the National Football Conference had held on the title since 1984. The Broncos came back the following year to win it all once again.

As always, big names dominated play on the gridiron. Fans cheered quarterback sensation Joe Montana during his last years at the helm of the San Francisco 49ers. In 1990, his last year with the team, he led them to another Super Bowl victory, winning the MVP award yet again. Dan Marino, quarterback for the Miami Dolphins, surpassed legendary quarterback Fran Tarkenton (Minnesota Vikings and New York Giants, 1961-78) in four passing categories: attempts, completions, yards, and touchdowns. Jerry Rice, wide receiver for the 49ers, established all-time records for catches and pass receiving yardage. Emmitt Smith, running back for the Cowboys, tallied twenty-five touchdowns in 1995, breaking the old standard. Barry Sanders, running back for the Detroit Lions, rushed for over one thousand yards in ten consecutive seasons (1989–98), setting an NFL record. Don Shula, longtime coach for both the Baltimore Colts (1963–69)

1990s Stanley Cup Champions

Year	Winning Team/Games Won	Losing Team/Games Won
1990	Edmonton Oilers 4	Boston Bruins 1
1991	Pittsburgh Penguins 4	Minnesota North Stars 2
1992	Pittsburgh Penguins 4	Chicago Black Hawks 0
1993	Montreal Canadiens 4	Los Angeles Kings 1
1994	New York Rangers 4	Vancouver Canucks 3
1995	New Jersey Devils 4	Detroit Red Wings 0
1996	Colorado Avalanche 4	Florida Panthers 0
1997	Detroit Red Wings 4	Philadelphia Flyers 0
1998	Detroit Red Wings 4	Washington Capitals 0
1999	Dallas Stars 4	Buffalo Sabres 2

and Miami Dolphins (1970–95), became the most winning coach in NFL history on November 14, 1993. When he retired after the 1995 season, Shula had led his teams to a record 347 victories.

❖ HOCKEY: U.S. EXPANSION

Much to the dismay of Canadian fans, their national sport moved south of the border in the 1990s as six new National Hockey League (NHL) franchises played in America's Sun Belt: San Jose Sharks (1991), Tampa Bay Lightning (1992), Anaheim Mighty Ducks (1993), Florida Panthers (1993), Nashville Predators (1998), and Atlanta Thrashers (1999). Only one traditional venue for hockey was added in the decade, the Ottawa Senators (1992). Having gained the Senators, Canada lost the Quebec Nordiques in 1995 when the team moved to Denver and became the Colorado Avalanche. At the same time, the Winnipeg Jets moved to Arizona where they became the Phoenix Coyotes. Completing the southern migration of major league hockey was the relocation of the Hartford Whalers to Raleigh, North Carolina, to become the Carolina Hurricanes. In 1999, one of the southern teams even won the Stanley Cup, the symbol of league supremacy, when the Dallas Stars beat the Buffalo Sabres four games to two.

Unfortunately, league expansion did not increase the number of talented recruits to the professional ranks. The results were apparent on the scoreboard. During the 1997–1998 season, teams scored only 5.3 goals per game, the lowest per-game average in the league in forty-two years. Four consecutive years of four-game sweeps (1995–98) in the Stanley Cup finals did nothing to help television ratings, which dropped 27 percent during the regular season and 22 percent during the playoffs. U.S. and Canadian talent often took a back seat to talented players imported from Russia, the Czech Republic, and Finland.

In a move to increase public awareness of hockey in the United States, in 1998 the NHL allowed a seventeen-day break from league play so its players could participate in the Olympics for the first time. Ironically, this break may have benefited the sport far more in other countries than in the United States. The Czech Republic team bested Russia for the gold medal in Nagano, Japan, after beating Canada in a huge upset in the semifinals. The U.S. team failed to win a medal and behaved badly off the ice, committing thousands of dollars worth of vandalism after losing to the Czechs by a score of four to one. In marked contrast, the U.S. women's hockey team behaved better than the men both off and on the ice, winning the gold medal at the same Olympiad.

Great players and coaches, some of whom retired during the decade, left their mark on the game. After a year as a free agent with the New York Rangers, Wayne Gretzky retired from hockey in 1999 at the age of thirty-eight. Although considered to be well past his prime, Gretzky still led the league in assists. During the 1997–98 season, he became the sixth player in NHL history to lead his team (the Rangers) in goals at age thirty-seven or older. Earlier in the decade, Gretzky led the league in assists in 1990,1991, 1992, and 1994. He won the Art Ross Trophy (1990, 1991, and 1994) for most points scored, calculated by adding goals and assists. Mario Lemieux of the Pittsburgh Penguins won the award four of the other seven years (1992, 1993, 1996, and 1997), and Jaromir Jagr (pronounced YAH-gur) of the Pittsburgh Penguins won the award the other three years (1995, 1998, and 1999). Unlike Gretzky, Scotty Bowman, the winningest coach in professional hockey, did not retire, but continued to win. With 1,300 career victories through the 1999 season, Bowman added three Stanley Cups to his resume (1992 with Pittsburgh, and 1997 and 1998 with Detroit), giving him a total of eight. No other coach, active or inactive, comes close to his numbers.

❖ GOLF: THE BEAR AND THE TIGER
Any discussion of professional golf in the second half of the twentieth century must include Jack Nicklaus. Even in his sixth decade, Nicklaus dominated the news from the Professional Golfers Association (PGA) and the talk on golf courses everywhere. Though he did not win a major golf

PGA Player of the Year in the 1990s

Year	Player
1990	Nick Faldo
1991	Corey Pavin
1992	Fred Couples
1993	Nick Price
1994	Nick Price
1995	Greg Norman
1996	Tom Lehman
1997	Tiger Woods
1998	Mark O'Meara
1999	Tiger Woods

tournament during the 1990s, Nicklaus, nicknamed the Golden Bear, kept things interesting and exciting in a variety of ways. He was on every all-sports, all-century list that came out during the decade. In 1998, he made the Masters Championship exciting with a Sunday charge that had him only two strokes off the lead on the front nine (the first nine of eighteen holes) on the final day of the tournament. He ended up in sixth place, only four strokes behind the winner. Finally, after 154 consecutive appearances in the major championships, Nicklaus declined to participate in the U.S. Open in 1998. His streak is unlikely to be broken.

As Nicklaus's star began to dim, another player, Tiger Woods, seemed to challenge the Golden Bear for the title of greatest golfer of the century. Indeed, no player other than Nicklaus had ever ruled the sport as Woods did toward the end of the 1990s. Woods's reign began when as a teenager he won the U.S. Amateur Championship each of three consecutive years (1994–96), becoming the first golfer in history to do so. In 1996, he also won the National Collegiate Athletic Association (NCAA) Championship. When he turned pro in September 1996, his first year of competition was better than the lifetime careers of most players. He won the fifth event he entered, the Las Vegas Invitational, and finished first in six of twenty-five events, breaking the single-season money record. Woods won the 1997 Masters by shooting an amazingly low eighteen-under-par score over seventy-two holes, twelve strokes better than his nearest competitor. He suffered a "sophomore slump" in 1998, yet still compiled a record that many golfers would envy, winning three events. Then in 1999, Woods returned to the top of his game, earning more than $6 million to set another record—more than doubling the annual winnings of any other golfer in history.

Although Woods dominated the headlines, many professional golfers played well during the decade. Hale Irwin won the U.S. Open (1990), three PGA Senior Championships (1996–98), the U.S. Senior Open (1998), and the Senior Players' Championship (1999). Three players each won the U.S. Open twice: Payne Stewart (1991 and 1999), Lee Janzen (1993 and 1998), and Ernie Els (1994 and 1997). Stewart's death in a plane crash in 1999, however, cut short his brilliant career. Mark O'Meara had a good year in 1998, winning both the Masters and the British Open. John Daly won two majors, the PGA (1991) and British Open (1995). Other players who won regularly and earned big money included Davis Love III, Fred Couples, Tom Kite, and David Duval. By the end of the decade, each had made more than $10 million in their careers.

Women's golf also had its bright stars. Betsy King began the 1990s the same way she finished the 1980s, winning two U.S. Women's Opens (1989 and 1990) and three Dinah Shore Classics (1987, 1990, 1997). These victories helped King become the all-time leading money winner on the women's tour with over six million dollars. Other multiple American winners in the major women's tournaments during the decade included Beth Daniel, Patty Sheehan, Meg Mallon, and Juli Inkster.

❖ **TENNIS: SAMPRAS'S DECADE**

Pete Sampras practically owned men's professional tennis during the 1990s. Sampras not only won six Wimbledon trophies (1993–95 and 1997–99), he also won the Australian Open twice (1994, 1997) and U.S. Open four times (1990, 1993, 1995, 1996). *Sports Illustrated* called him the best male tennis player of the century when he edged out Bill Tilden, whose glory years were in the 1920s. At the end of the decade, Sampras had won 61 career titles and spent more weeks (276) as the top-ranked player than anyone in history.

The fortunes of other Americans playing professional tennis were much more erratic. Andre Agassi was both hot and cold during the decade, winning five Grand Slam events: Wimbledon (1992), the U.S. Open (1994, 1999), the Australian Open (1995), and the French Open (1999). Other American men who had a memorable decade included Jim Courier and

Sports Illustrated *named Pete Sampras the best male tennis player of the century.* **Reproduced by permission of AP/Wide World Photos.**

U.S. Open Tennis Tournament Champions

Year	Male	Female
1990	Pete Sampras	Gabriela Sabatini
1991	Stefan Edberg	Monica Seles
1992	Stefan Edberg	Monica Seles
1993	Pete Sampras	Steffi Graf
1994	Andre Agassi	Arantxa Sanchez Vicario
1995	Pete Sampras	Steffi Graf
1996	Pete Sampras	Steffi Graf
1997	Patrick Rafter	Martina Hingis
1998	Patrick Rafter	Lindsey Davenport
1999	Andre Agassi	Serena Williams

Michael Chang. Courier won twice in Australia (1992 and 1993) and twice in France (1991 and 1992). Chang is one of only three American men to earn at least $15 million in career winnings, along with Sampras ($35 million) and Agassi ($15 million).

On the women's professional tour, Monica Seles, Lindsay Davenport, and the Williams sisters, Venus and Serena, all took center stage. Davenport won the titles in the 1996 Olympics, U.S. Open (1998), and Wimbledon (1999). Seles won nine Grand Slam events, but had to endure time off the court at the peak of her career after being stabbed by a fan of her rival, Steffi Graf, in 1993. Having already won the Australian Open (1991–93), the French Open (1990–92), and the U.S. Open (1991–92), Seles spent a significant portion of the next three years recovering from her stab wounds. Remarkably, she returned to the Women's Tennis Association (WTA) Tour with a win at the Canadian Open in 1995 and reclaimed the Australian Open title in 1996. Venus and Serena Williams were rising stars, with Venus claiming nine singles titles before the end of the decade and Serena claiming her first Gland Slam title, the U.S. Open, in 1999.

❖ THE OLYMPICS

The 1992 Winter Olympics, held in Albertville, France, featured 1,313 male and 488 female athletes representing 64 nations. It was the first

Olympiad after the end of the cold war, the period of extreme political tension between the United States and the former Soviet Union after World War II (1939–45). The breakup of the former Soviet Union, which had begun in the late 1980s, and the dismantling of the Berlin Wall (1989) affected the Olympics as countries such as Lithuania, Estonia, and Latvia competed under their own flags for the first time since before World War II. Germany sent one team instead of two (since East and West Germany had reunited), and some former Soviet athletes competed under the United Team name.

Athletes from the United States won five gold medals, four silver medals, and two bronze medals in Albertville, placing the team fifth in the overall medal count. Americans won two medals in the showcase event of women's figure skating, where Kristi Yamaguchi, the favorite, won the gold, and Nancy Kerrigan won the bronze. The other U.S. Olympic star in Albertville was speed skater Bonnie Blair, who won gold in the women's 500- and 1,000-meter races.

In the summer games held that year in Barcelona, Spain, 169 nations were represented by 9,367 athletes (6,659 men and 2,708 women). Politics seemed to matter less than in previous years as Cuba, North Korea, and Ethiopia ended their boycotts, with each nation having missed two Olympic games. South Africa, which had been absent since 1960 because of its government-sponsored racial-discriminatory policy of apartheid, also returned to competition.

Many American athletes competed in Barcelona with considerable distinction but some failed to meet expectations. The basketball Dream Team, made up of National Basketball Association (NBA) all-stars (the first time professionals were allowed to represent the United States in basketball) swept easily to a gold medal. The baseball team, however, managed only a fourth-place finish in the new Olympic sport. Overall, the U.S. Olympic team won gold medals in thirty-seven events, second only to the Unified Team in the gold-medal count. American athletes also took home thirty-four silver medals and thirty-seven bronze medals. Track and field star Carl Lewis continued to strengthen his claim during the 1990s as the outstanding male Summer Olympic athlete of the century. Lewis became one of only two individuals ever to win nine Olympic gold medals in track and field. Jesse Owens, along with Lewis, became the only two athletes to win four gold medals in the same event. Although affected by a virus during the1992 Olympics, Lewis was still able to win gold in the long jump, a feat he also achieved in 1984, 1988, and 1996. Jackie Joyner-Kersee was chosen as the outstanding female Summer Olympian of the century. During the 1992 Olympics, she followed up on her two track and field gold medals (heptathlon and long jump) from the previous Olympics by winning the gold in the seven-event heptathlon.

Beginning in 1994, the International Olympic Committee (the governing body of the Olympics) decided the Winter and Summer Olympics would no longer be held in the same year every four years, but would be staggered and held two years apart. The winter games were held that year in Lillehammer, Norway, and 1,217 male and 522 female athletes from 67 countries competed. Americans won six gold medals in essentially the same events as they had in 1992. Figure skater Nancy Kerrigan, who had been assaulted while preparing for the U.S. figure skating championships only a month earlier (her rival Tonya Harding was implicated in the affair), turned in a silver-medal performance. Another repeat performer from the 1992 Winter Olympics was Bonnie Blair, who was competing in her fourth Olympiad. Again, she won the women's 500-meter and 1,000-meter races, bringing her total number of Olympic victories to five. Fellow speed skater Dan Jansen took gold in the men's

American speedskater Bonnie Blair won the gold medal in the 1992 Winter Olympics in Albertville, France. Reproduced by permission of AP/Wide World Photos.

1,000-meter race. In Alpine skiing, Tommy Moe won the men's downhill while Picabo (pronounced PEEK-ah-boo) Street took a silver medal in the women's event.

The 1996 Summer Olympics in Atlanta, Georgia, hosted 10,320 athletes (6,797 men and 3,523 women) from 197 countries. Tragedy struck the games when a homemade bomb exploded on July 27 in the Olympic Centennial Park, killing one woman and injuring 110. The games continued, following the precedent established by International Olympic Committee during the 1972 Summer Olympics, when eleven Israeli athletes were taken hostage and later murdered by terrorists, the games continued.

In the competition venues, U.S. athletes shone, winning forty-four gold, thirty-two silver, and twenty-five bronze medals. Probably the most thrilling American competitors were the members of the women's gymnastics team. Shannon Miller won the gold with her prowess on the beam, and the team won the gold medal with a gutsy performance, especially by the injured Kerri Strug, who made her last vault landing on a badly sprained ankle. In track-and-field events, Michael Johnson won both the men's 200- and 400-meter races, a first in Olympic history. Gail Devers won her second consecutive gold medal in the women's 100-meter race. And Carl Lewis won gold in the long jump, becoming only the fourth person in history ever to win the same individual event four times. The American women's swim team again dominated the pool, winning seven golds, five silvers, and three bronzes. The men's swim team was not far behind with thirteen total medals, six of them gold. The U.S. women's soccer team won their event, a prelude to winning the World Cup in 1999. Both victories gave women's athletics a boost in the United States.

The final Olympic games of the twentieth century were the 1998 Winter Olympics held in Nagano, Japan, with 1,488 male and 814 female athletes from 72 nations competing. Once again, the U.S. team won six gold medals in winter events. With professional hockey players allowed to compete for the first time, the U.S. team disappointed the country on and off the ice. They lost an important match to the Czech Republic four to one, then trashed three Olympic apartments in a display of unsportsmanlike conduct. The women's hockey team redeemed the sport by winning the gold in their debut event. Skier Picabo Street returned to the podium, this time receiving the gold medal for her victory in the women's super giant slalom event. One delightful surprise was the gold medal performance of fifteen-year-old Tara Lipinski in women's figure skating. With her victory, she became the youngest champion in an individual event in the history of the Winter Olympics.

✦ For More Information

BOOKS

Armstrong, Lance, with Sally Jenkins. *It's Not About the Bike: My Journey Back to Life*. New York: Putnam, 2000.

Jordan, Michael. *For the Love of the Game: My Story*. Edited by Mark Vancil. New York: Crown Publishers, 1998.

Miller, Calvin Craig. *Pete Sampras*. Greensboro, NC: Morgan Reynolds, 1998.

Miller, Marla. *All American Girls: The U.S. Women's National Soccer Team*. New York: Pocket Books, 1999.

Muscat, Carrie. *Mark McGwire*. Philadelphia, PA: Chelsea House Publishing, 1999.

Stout, Glenn, ed. *Chasing Tiger: The Tiger Woods Reader*. Cambridge, MA: De Capo Press, 2002.

Summitt, Pat, with Sally Jenkins. *Raise the Roof: The Inspiring Inside Story of the Tennessee Lady Vols' Undefeated 1997-98 Season*. New York: Broadway Books, 1998.

WEB SITES

LPGA Official Website. http://www.lpga.com/ (accessed on May 29, 2002).

NBA.com http://www.nba.com (accessed on May 29, 2002).

NFL.com. http://www.nfl.com/ (accessed on May 29, 2002).

NHL.com-The National Hockey League Web Site. http://www.nhl.com (accessed on May 29, 2002).

The Official Site of Major League Baseball. http://mlb.mlb.com/NASApp/mlb/mlb/homepage/mlb_homepage.jsp (accessed on May 29, 2002).

The Official Website of the Olympic Movement. http://www.olympic.org/uk/index_uk.asp (accessed on May 29, 2002).

PGA of America. http://www.pga.com/ (accessed on May 29, 2002).

Tour de France. http://www.letour.fr/indexus.html (accessed on May 29, 2002).

United States Tennis Association. http://www.usta.com/index.html (accessed on May 29, 2002).

Where to Learn More

BOOKS

Condon, Judith. *The Nineties*. Austin, TX: Raintree/Steck-Vaughn, 2000.

Feinstein, Stephen. *The 1990s: From the Persian Gulf War to Y2K*. Berkeley Heights, NJ: Enslow, 2001.

Haley, James, ed. *Post-Cold War America: 1992-Present*. San Diego, CA: Greenhaven Press, 2003.

Kallen, Stuart A., ed. *The 1990s*. San Diego, CA: Greenhaven Press, 2000.

London, Herbert Ira. *Decade of Denial: A Snapshot of America in the 1990s*. Lanham, MD: Lexington Books, 2001.

Time-Life Books, ed. *The Digital Decade: The 90s*. Alexandria, VA: 2000.

WEB SITES

American Cultural History: 1990–1999. http://www.nhmccd.cc.tx.us/contracts/lrc/kc/decade90.html (accessed on June 1, 2002).

Biography of America: Contemporary History. http://www.learner.org/biographyofamerica/prog25/index.html (accessed on June 1, 2002).

1860–2000 General History: 1990s. http://cdcga.org/HTMLs/decades/1990s.htm (accessed on June 1, 2002).

History Channel. http://www.historychannel.com/index.html (accessed on June 1, 2002).

HyperHistory Online. http://www.hyperhistory.com/online_n2/History_n2/a.html (accessed on June 1, 2002).

In the 90s: the Nineties Nostalgia Site. http://www.inthe90s.com/index.shtml (accessed on June 1, 2002).

Where to Learn More

Map: Political Systems of the World in the 1990s. http://users.erols.com/mwhite28/govt1990.htm (accessed on June 1, 2002).

Media History Timeline: 1990s. http://www.mediahistory.umn.edu/time/1990s.html (accessed on June 1, 2002).

1990s Flashback: 1990–1999. http://www.1990sflashback.com/ (accessed on June 1, 2002).

Nobel e-Museum. http://www.nobel.se/ (accessed June 1, 2002).

Official Website of the Olympic Movement. http://www.olympic.org/uk/index_uk.asp (accessed on June 1, 2002).

20th Century American Culture. http://members.aol.com/TeacherNet/20CC.html (accessed on June 1, 2002).

20th Century Decades: 1990–1999 Decade. http://dewey.chs.chico.k12.ca.us/decs9.html (accessed on June 1, 2002).

20th Century Fashion History: 1980s–1990s. http://www.costumegallery.com/1980.htm (accessed on June 1, 2002).

20th Century History. http://history1900s.about.com/ (accessed on June 1, 2002).

Index